The Disease of MORE

One Woman's 25-Year Recovery from Alcoholism and Food Addiction

Eleanor R.

TAKE CHARGE BOOKS

Brevard, North Carolina

Take Charge Books
PO Box 1452
Brevard, NC 28712

Library of Congress Cataloging-in Publication Data:

LCCN # 2011920061

ISBN 978-0-9815818-3-5

Editor: Kathleen Barnes
Typesetting/graphic design: Gary A. Rosenberg
Cover design: Gary A. Rosenberg

Printed in the United States of America

10   9   8   7   6   5   4   3   2   1

Contents

*This book is dedicated
to my father and my mother
who showed me The Way.*

Introduction

I wrote this book to share my experiences, my strength and hope through my journey to become the woman I always wanted to be. I cannot use my full name because that would violate the traditions of Alcoholics Anonymous, which requires that I not reveal my identity when carrying this message of recovery at the public level.

My recovery has manifested in great personal and professional success. I am not allowed to use my position to sell books or to glorify myself in anyway, but I can say I have a successful career as a public servant in one of the largest states in the nation. Ultimately, it is simply better that I remain anonymous so that I do not forget that this book is really not about me anyway. It is about sharing a story that shows that anyone can be relieved of the disease of addiction: The Disease of More. Even I, a hopeless, helpless, stumbling, fearful, willful and always right, human being can follow simple directions and emerge changed for the better.

This book is for those who suffer from substance abuse and for those with loved ones who suffer from substance abuse. I have found that this definition includes most of us.

My particular loves were alcohol and food. But I have also acted in an addicted manner to people, gum, shopping, diet sodas, television, computer use, artificial sweetener and salt. I have this thing in my brain that tells me that if a little feels good or tastes good, more must be better. I tell myself that more must be better and I proceed to follow that edict into the gates of hell.

I followed it until I became so sick, bloated, broke, broken, drunk and/or isolated that I suffered in a manner that led me to want to do insane things: like divorce my perfectly amazing husband, quit my amazing and powerful career, leave the country, take LSD "just for the experience," leave my whole family and start over like a witness protection candidate, have love affairs with motorcycle outlaws, kill myself and/or shave my head and move to Tibet, just to mention a few.

I hope that you will enjoy the lessons I have learned that I've shared with you in this book. It has been a labor of love. I also hope that you may find peace in some of the passages and experiences and realize that happiness is possible for everyone.

Eleanor R.
December 2010

THE TWELVE STEPS OF ALCOHOLICS ANONYMOUS

1. We admitted we were powerless over alcohol—that our lives had become unmanageable.

2. Came to believe that a Power greater than ourselves could restore us to sanity.

3. Made a decision to turn our will and our lives over to the care of God *as we understood Him.*

4. Made a searching and fearless moral inventory of ourselves.

5. Admitted to God, to ourselves, and to another human being the exact nature of our wrongs.

6. Were entirely ready to have God remove all these defects of character.

7. Humbly asked Him to remove our shortcomings.

8. Made a list of all persons we had harmed, and became willing to make amends to them all.

9. Made direct amends to such people wherever possible, except when to do so would injure them or others.

10. Continued to take personal inventory and when we were wrong promptly admitted it.

11. Sought through prayer and meditation to improve our conscious contact with God, *as we understood Him,* praying only for knowledge of His will for us and the power to carry that out.

12. Having had a spiritual awakening as the result of these Steps, we tried to carry this message to alcoholics, and to practice these principles in all our affairs.

—Copyright © A.A. World Services, Inc.

CHAPTER I

· · · · · · · · · · · ·

The Backstory

I was raised in the 12 Steps of Alcoholics Anonymous. My mother has been going to Alanon since I was two years old because my father was a falling down, sometimes violent drunk. My mother knew almost from the beginning that I was also likely to be an alcoholic. She would lecture me about how I was "just like my father." She told me that I was self-centered, selfish, stubborn and never thought of others. My mother coped the best she could, but she saw the writing on the wall and she couldn't help but break into the occasional diatribe about how I was just like him.

I remember thinking to myself, "Is that a good thing or a bad thing?" I was seven.

My father was in and out of the rooms of Alcoholics Anonymous. He got sober and then he would drink, go to jail, get sober, drink and get arrested again. I am pretty sure that Mom knew I was an alcoholic long before I took my first drink because I had all the early symptoms: sugar cravings, irritability, extreme self-centeredness, genetics and a chaotic home life.

I really do think my mother knew that it was only a matter of time before I would have to attend a 12-Step program and that she began praying for me early. I am pretty sure that while other mothers were praying that their children would finish high school and get into a decent college that my mother was praying that I lived through high school without getting arrested or pregnant. That is definitely the kind of kid I was. I was so involved in my disease at such a young age that just surviving adolescence was a miracle. My mom told me that she prayed I would find AA for myself and luckily, I did before too much damage was done.

Regrettably, my father was a mean drunk. He was a really nice guy though—when he was not drinking—so I was confused for much of my childhood. I loved my father more than life itself. He was so big and strong. He was like Hercules to me. I felt so small in the shadow of his bicep or his enormous muscle-bound thigh. He was also physically beautiful and funny. When I was a very little girl, I was in love with my father for what seemed like years. I would often ask him why he did not wait for me to grow up so that I could marry him.

He would answer me very directly, "If I had not married your mother, we would never have had you."

I had no idea what he was talking about, but I settled for that answer over and over again as odd as it seemed to me at the age of four.

Even though I knew that my father was a mean drunk, I worshipped him. I am my father's daughter through and through. I adored him and I sought his approval until the day he died. The first time he told me he loved me (that I recall), I was 23 years old. I called him from the East, where I had just registered to attend law school. He most likely told me that he loved me when I was a small child, because I remember him loving me as much as I loved him, but I hadn't *heard* it until that moment.

A lot happened, however, between the ages of 4 and 23, so I seemed to have developed some sort of amnesia about his love for me for almost two decades throughout adolescence and young adulthood. Between the ages of 4 and 23, I wanted him to hold me and tell me he loved me, but it was just too hard for him. I built walls around my heart from an early age due to the chaos and the environment of extreme dysfunction that we called our home.

My parents were 17 and 19 when they married. My mother was pregnant with my brother. As an adult, I learned that he was conceived in the back seat of a '57 Chevy while they were on a date. I was devastated because before that moment I thought my mother was the Virgin Mary. After my mother got pregnant, she dropped out of high school. My father was a record-making high school football player who was scouted by the pros and won a scholarship to a junior college in the Bay Area of California. My mother was never accepted into my father's family and my father's mother accused her of stealing away my father's football career. Later in life, my father would admit that it was not my mother, but alcoholism that stole away his football career.

Such were the humble beginnings of my parents: A high school dropout and a community college dropout living in Section 8 housing. Both of my parents' families were large. Both families were farm workers and factory workers. The family secrets and dysfunction from both sides were significant and the level of protection of those family secrets ran deep. I was informed much later in life that both my great-grandfathers on my father's side (who were brothers because my grandmother and grandfather were first cousins) were killed in bar fights in Mexico. That was the context of my birth.

My earliest memories are of scooting around on my bottom because I could not walk when most toddlers begin to walk. We lived on College Street in a rural agricultural town in the middle of California, the place of my birth. The little white house perched on one of the main residential streets was a mansion to me. Years later when I went to see it, it was a small cottage no more than eight or nine hundred square feet. I have very fond memories of the little white house even though my mother tells me that we were there for only a short time when I was ages two and three.

There was a very kind woman named Elizabeth who lived next door. She was African-American and the most beautiful woman that I had ever seen. She was regal and perfectly coifed. She also let me dip into the candy dish whenever I visited. Today I know that I must have "scooted" over, up the front steps to the front door. There was no other way I could have made my way to her house. My brother, just about a year older than me, was always with me.

My mother tells me that she used to stand me up to help me learn to walk. But she said that rather than be excited about trying to walk, I would cry. When she realized that I was in too much pain to try to learn to walk, she took me to the doctor. The doctor said I was fine and that I was a late walker. My mother said she knew differently. She knew that I might never walk if she did not find another doctor to help me. She also told me that no one took her seriously since she was a poor Mexican teenaged mother on public aid.

She called the March of Dimes out of desperation, hoping for financial assistance, however, the March of Dimes would not help. She found a doctor about 20 miles east of our little rural town who finally did some tests on me and learned that my hip socket was not properly forming and that I would need considerable treatment and physical therapy. I had to wear special shoes that had a bar between them so that my hip and leg joints could be held in place while I grew. I was not able to walk for some time and when I did, I still had to wear leg braces and orthopedic shoes. I know today that I felt different from the other kids from the start and that perhaps this was part of it.

The orthopedic shoes were clunky and white. I never got to wear sparkly Dorothy shoes or black patent Mary Janes. From my adult love of beautiful clothes, I know I would have loved to wear such girly shoes and I am sad that I missed out. We were also never allowed to give donations to the March of Dimes after their rejection of my family.

My mother also describes me at this time as a child who would not take a nap. She and my brother would go down for a nap without me. My mother would put me in the highchair with a stack of Oreos while she and my brother slept. She said that I was perfectly content when they woke up. I did not make a sound and I was still busy eating my cookies. When she told me this story, it seemed funny. But now it just makes me sad. I know that my mother did the best she could, but I cannot help but see how this way of dealing with me at the age of two or three shaped my place in the family.

Even at that young age, I was seen as self-sufficient and not in need of much "nurturing." I can also see that I started using substances really early—sugar in this case—to keep me occupied and content, rather than connect with loving human beings.

My father's alcoholism caused our family to be thrown into a variety of situations that I am certain other children do not experience. I remember visiting him at "work" on the weekends. It was actually jail where my father was allowed to do yard work at the jail wearing a bright orange jump suit. We would drive by, say hello, give him some food and leave. I think now, knowing what I know about the criminal justice system, that he must have been doing some sort of weekend work program as a jail sentence. I cannot imagine today that anyone's family would be able to drive by and give a jail inmate lunch, but that is what we did then.

I remember watching *Mayberry RFD* and having great compassion for Otis, the town drunk. I later realized that my father was the town drunk. I was always so happy when Otis would sober up. I was always so happy when my father did not drink. He would not drink for stretches at a time. Everything was different when he was sober. The atmosphere was lighter; we were all happier.

But I also know that I waited. I was a vigilant child and I knew intuitively that the monster would be back. It was just a matter of when.

Even when I was a very young child, I saw and felt the heaviness of a family being torn apart by alcoholism. I say that I felt it because when I was so young, I just did not have words. What I did have was really bad childhood eczema. I had an awful, itchy, scabbing skin rash all over my hands and feet for years. It was agony for a child who just wanted to be the same as everyone else. I was teased by other children because of the obvious skin deformity that caused big scabby blisters and redness on my fingers and toes. I had to soak my feet in purple medicated water, so my extremities were also very purplish instead of the beautiful smooth brown skin that I have today. As an adult, I have researched the causes of eczema and learned that stress is a key factor. I believe I wore my family dysfunction in that physical manifestation.

In my profession today, when I see children coming from families with the chaos of addiction, I immediately recommend mental health counseling so that the child can at least begin to verbalize the pain that he or she is suffering in order to mitigate and heal the physical as well as the mental and spiritual. I also do a high five to my Higher Power thanking the Universe for my personal experience so that I can help another child in a not-so-conventional way.

I loved my brother and two sisters. I was their little mommy. My brother Peter was just a bit older and he was the light of my life. He was kind, loving, physically beautiful and funny. He took care to make sure that we spent time together, especially when I was suffering from the eczema and the house was full of tension and instability.

My sister Kay came along when I was five. My mother used to call her the "Pill Baby" because apparently she was on the pill and still got pregnant. I was so happy when Kay came home from the hospital. She had a full head of black hair and milky white skin. We used to say that she was brought by the milkman because she was so fair. She also mostly wore a frown and had to be really coddled to crack a smile.

She was born at one of the most stressful times in our family. We were living in Section 8 housing and my Mother was spread really thin. My father was working at a rice mill and everything felt hard.

Next came my sister Claire, six years later. She was joy embodied. She was a happy baby and at age six or seven I was happy to take care of her. I lost myself in loving her.

As a very young child, I was sexually assaulted many times by an extended family member. I became vigilant, shut down and afraid inside, but I was tough and sucked it up on the outside. I would say I was six or seven years old when the abuse stopped. I never told anyone about the serial sexual assaults, although I am not sure why. I just tolerated them and made sure that my abuser did not hurt my sisters. Everything about my life was inconsistent. I behaved well and felt loved, but I also felt afraid, hypervigilant and sometimes out of control.

As the girls grew and my father's drinking grew worse, I became more and more the protector and nurturer to my siblings. We girls all shared a room for years. When I was fifteen and we got our first home and our own bedrooms, we still all slept in my bed for months because we did not want to be without each other. I sang to them and read them to sleep each night. We said prayers and I kissed them and hugged them before putting myself to bed. That was a lovely, stressful time.

CHAPTER 2

The Wild Years

Dr. Clarissa Pinkola Estes writes that women possess an instinctual nature or wildness and that societal attempts to domesticate them are oppressive and result in the suppression of their spiritual lives, ultimately killing intuition and contact with the spirit world. I entirely identify with this insight. I have always had a superior instinctual nature and, from my earliest memories, I have had a wild nature that rejects efforts at conformity. I had no idea what to do with this gift. I had no one to affirm my keen instinctual nature and nurture it into its fullness to serve the universe, so I felt boxed in and I rebelled.

I was born in a small rural country county in the middle of California. There were few choices for Latinas back in the sixties. My mother was terrified I would end up like her and my father wanted me to leave his house and get married as soon as I finished high school. But I had other plans. When I was about 11 or 12, I read books about women who lived in big cities like New York and were independent and had careers. Very early, I formulated a burning desire to go away and see the big cities of the United States as soon as I could.

As I grew up and went through puberty, my relationship with my father became strained. While he was great with small children, he was not so great with teen girls. He would get drunk and violent with my mother. We would all hide and the next day he would pretend nothing happened. His family was from Mexico, so he had many old school standards about how girls should behave. He was terribly oppressive towards my mother and, by default, to all of his daughters.

Reading was my escape. I read constantly and I read everything. The more I read, the more I realized that I wanted much more than my father could ever imagine for one of his girl-children. My brother, the firstborn, was the family jewel and the world was touted as his oyster. The girls were treated differently: They were to be seen and not heard. Such is the legacy of the new immigrant, the unenlightened Mexican patriarch. Nevertheless, as time marched on, I adored and feared my father and ultimately, in spite of my extremely anxious attachment, I desperately needed and sought his approval while I lived what came to be a double life.

I call it a double life because I simultaneously learned how to please my father with obedient behavior, but inside I was a wild child, a wild teenager and, ultimately a wild woman. Like all good addicts from day one, I had learned to be devious in order to be wild. I had always been pulled towards the dark side of life. I wanted to go to parties and drink and smoke, work in an exciting and dangerous profession and have painfully romantic affairs with older men.

From a very young age, I wanted to live large and color outside the lines. Even though I wanted to live large, I felt like I was in a box. I felt suffocated and oppressed by the role of being the oldest girl in a Mexican family with lots of responsibility and no instruction.

I do not think I was mourning my lost childhood back then. I definitely mourned later when I had kids, but here I had become parentified: I had become a child who acts like the parent, a child who had to act like a grownup with no real guidance on how to be a grownup. I had a child's mind along with incredible burdens inappropriate for a child; I did not possess the consciousness to be in mourning for a childhood that was never to be.

Very early in life, I developed the Disease of More.

From the very start, I couldn't get enough of any substance that changed the way I felt. As a school-aged child, I would come home to an empty house and gorge myself on saltine crackers and butter. I would eat whatever I could without getting in trouble.

I graduated from saltine cracker gorges at nine or ten to bulimia by the age of 15. From there, food addiction became a lifelong struggle. I was bulimic for nine torturous years. At my worst, I would drive to the store several times a day to stock up on binge foods— salty, crunchy, sweet, creamy and spicy. I would come home and eat everything in secret until it hurt. I would go into the bathroom, put my finger down my throat and throw everything up. I would vomit until bile was coming out so then I knew I would not gain weight. Then I would do it again.

"This one last time," I would tell myself. I would drive to the store again and get another set of binge foods: salty, sweet, crunchy and smooth. Back to the house to a secret binge and back to the bathroom to kneel at the toilet bowl to unleash the evil substance that would cause weight gain.

I was really young when I started to drink alcohol. I remember a "family function" where they had a champagne fountain that even the kids were allowed to "taste." In those days we had lots of huge family parties. The parties were so big we rented halls. I remember family reunions, anniversaries, birthday celebrations and weddings.

Everything was big: The cake was big, the food was big, the dresses were big and the music and the drinks ran through the party like we were in a Cecil B. DeMille film. Mariachi bands in their grand costumes played the music of the old country and women made fresh tortillas and served them up warm with beans, rice and pork or chicken. The smells were heavenly! No one paid much attention to the children as we ran around in packs unattended to make whatever mischief we could imagine.

I got drunk for the first time at the age of nine or ten. I remember loving that feeling of being transported out of my insecure body to a feeling where everything was okay and I was beautiful just like my slightly older cousins with their store bought dresses and perfectly coifed hair.

Such was the launching of the alcoholic/bulimic first girl child of my father. Later in life, my brother would get sober long before me and one of my sisters made her commitment to sobriety when she was 20, six months after I hit my bottom.

So I lived hard just like my Dad. I suffered the consequences in spades, just like my Dad. And just like my Dad, I first attempted to get sober in my early 20s. He was my trailblazer and he didn't even know it.

I started my delinquent behavior early. I began stealing candy from the corner store in elementary school with all my 4th grade friends. We would pack in after school and create a half moon around the penny candy and stuff our pockets. I know that the storeowner must have known we were stealing. Or maybe he didn't, since we were, after all, only 9 or 10 years old. We were cute and small so maybe he did not think that we were totally ripping him off. Or maybe he did not care and would chalk it up as the cost of doing business.

This time of candy stealing was the time that I consciously remember starting to feel bad. I was experiencing the Disease of More at this young age and I believed I did not have enough in spite of all evidence to the contrary: family, shelter, etc. My personhood was in dire straits before the age of 11!

I got through preadolescence because of one man, Mr. Stevens. He was my teacher for grades 4, 5 and 6. Mr. Stevens loved me. He loved me through a time of great upheaval in my life. He loved me during a time when my father was very ill with his alcoholism and my mother worked long hours outside the home to make ends meet. I was a latchkey child through these years and was basically raising myself; hence the ability to go to the drug store unsupervised after school and steal my brains out.

Mr. Stevens had a twinkle in his eye and he kept track of me.

He reminded me of St. Nicholas with his jolly disposition and his magical kindness. One day, I recall coming to school with makeup on. I had probably stolen some makeup from the drug store because I do not know where else I would have gotten it. We did graduate to stealing personal hygiene items by the sixth grade.

Anyway, I came to school one morning with blue eye shadow on my eyelids. Mr. Stevens took me into the girl's bathroom and washed it off. Wow! Today he would probably never have done that, but I needed to be fathered and I will be forever grateful to Mr. Stevens for loving me so much as to help me act right at such a young age. He praised me. He told me I was brilliant and he saw my good spirit. He saw my god-self, even though by the time I left him at the age of 12, it was already buried deep beneath the pain and struggle of life from all that was happening at home: the alcoholism, the domestic violence and the chaos.

I am certain however, if Mr. Stevens had not been there with me for those three years that I would not be where I am today. Although, at that time I was very far from the bottom and I had a very long and painful fall still ahead of me, but Mr. Stevens changed the trajectory of my life with his unconditional love and his work outside of his role as teacher to be a light in my life for all time.

I started junior high school at age 12 and was soon immersed in a world of sex, drugs and rock and roll. I was so young and vulnerable. I had an older brother, which meant that he had older friends. We spent a lot of time together and I began experimenting with mood altering substances and teenage sex, even before I was technically a teenager.

Unfortunately for me, I am my father's daughter in every way, so my addiction to alcohol was lying in wait. A lush was born the moment I took that first drink. Soon to follow was the high-risk and humiliating behavior and then the outright criminal behavior and a trail of broken hearts, not in the least, my own.

My family really did not know what was happening to me. I was left unattended for hours at a time and sometimes allowed to stay with friends overnight where there was no adult supervision. We smoked cigarettes and hustled or stole beer. We had no sense of the law as far as I could recall. We just wanted to have the warped teenaged version of "fun." I chased booze and boys from about ages 12 to 18 to the exclusion of almost everything else. I was up and down and thought I was having the time of my life. I did not realize that I was just as the statistics would have predicted: A textbook case of an adolescent girl who had suffered severe early childhood trauma whose was only mission was to self-medicate and engage in high-risk behavior (a form of self-medication).

CHAPTER 3

• • • • • • • • • • • • •

The Downward Slide and Hitting Bottom

Although I was bulimic and alcoholic, I somehow made it through high school. But high school was miserable. I didn't fit in. I was depressed and addicted. Looking back, I realize I did the best I could under the circumstances. Upon reflection, I have a great deal of compassion for that lost girl.

I hung out with a bunch of girls who came from similar home lives. Child neglect and abuse, divorce, drug and alcohol abuse and instability marked all of our lives.

Although my parents never divorced, they split up for long periods of time during my childhood. My heart broke each time my father moved out of the house. I was four the first time he left. I couldn't understand why he didn't live with us anymore. I was nine or ten the second time my father left. I was devastated. It was then that I began to blame my mother for our family misery. For many years, I hated her for kicking my father out of the house, even though in hindsight I now know it was the right thing to do.

So I tolerated high school. In spite of my active dual addictions to food and alcohol, I was captain of the field hockey team and co-starred in musical community theatre. I lost myself in activity. I was rarely home during the high school years. I was always out at practice for sports or rehearsal for drama and singing.

Throughout high school, I got drunk as often as possible and regularly humiliated myself at house and street parties. I went to many college parties at the local university and I was involved in extremely risky behavior. I would start out the evening drinking with my best friends and by the end of the night I would find myself with strange boys/men, in cars speeding to the next party or apartment for more booze and end up at the mercy of whoever I was "with" for the night. I really thought that I was having fun.

Afterwards, I always felt shame and guilt. I was a black/brownout drinker and I thought everyone else was too. I never really knew what I had done or said when I was under the influence and I was happy to leave those memories in the murk.

I left home as soon as I was allowed. I turned 18 in January of 1980, but I was not allowed to leave until after I graduated from high school later that year. I left the day after I graduated from high school and I never returned to live with my family again. As I was leaving, my father told me that I would be back. By then, our relationship was completely estranged. He was at a loss on how to deal with an out-of-control teen girl and I felt that he was oppressive and did not understand how intelligent I was.

Like all good addicts, I had big dreams at the age of 18. I can safely say that I was full of myself. I had delusions of grandeur coupled with an inferiority complex. I was involved with lots of different boys and men. I always had a boyfriend. I was very promiscuous and was unable to engage in any relationships that lasted more than a month. My relationships were more like one night stands that I obsessed over for 30 days before I'd move on when the glow wore off.

I literally "got through" college. But, in spite of my pathetic state of alcohol and food addiction, I began to tune into two important things: I wanted to be more than what I was and I started to see role models in others.

All those books that I read were still inside of me. I knew that I could have a better life. I learned something from being in the rooms of Alcoholics Anonymous for my whole life growing up while my father tried to get sober and my mother tried to get sane. I wanted more. However, since I was still crazy and my behavior was unpredictable, it was "more" in an undisciplined manner. I had plenty of zeal, but no wisdom or ability to reflect and calibrate. I ran headlong into life and smack in the middle of my disease. Most of my vision was self-centered and self-serving.

The first time I rode an airplane was just for a short hop and it was glorious! At the age of 22, I'd been sent on a business trip for some lobby work that I was doing as a student for the university. It was in a small two-engine prop plane.

The next trip, I flew across the country to do an internship in Washington, D.C., sight unseen. This time the plane was a huge Boeing 747. In one of my few memorable conversations with my father, he told me that it would be the first of many trips across the country. He was right. I lived in Washington, D.C. at 23 and worked for a couple of well-known peace and justice organizations in pursuit of my dream to become a member of Congress.

I consciously vowed that I would never be like my father. He was a weekend beer drunk. He usually drank away from the house. Now, I know that my mother most likely forbade alcohol in the house. She had grown up with an alcoholic father herself. I remember my grandmother telling all the kids "not to let Grandpa drink." She seemed so serious and would let us know on the down low to be alert for this house law violation. I got the feeling I was to tell her immediately if I ever saw liquor touch his lips. So I learned really early to have vigilance about alcohol.

The few times I did see my father drunk, he was a stumbling, falling down drunk. I saw him fall down a flight of stairs when we lived in a low-income apartment building when I was 3 or 4 years old. It made me scared.

It did not help that my mother was really emotionally ill during my preschool years. She would make us eat everything on our plates in the midst of the tensest atmosphere one could imagine with two young emotionally ill parents. I did everything I could to not cause trouble. So I pretended to eat and then coughed to put the yucky meat loaf in my napkin. Even at such a young age, food was playing a role in my effort to cope.

Oddly enough (or perhaps predictably) I got through college, barely. I was drunk every weekend. I had certain personal "rules" and I had broken all of them:

- Never drink alone: Did it.

- Never drink in the morning: Did it (and it was great, unfortunately).

- Never drink and drive: Did it.

- Never sleep with a married man: Did it.

I thought I was the life of the party, but actually I was the throwing-up slob in the bathroom who was just as likely to pass out in your hallway as steal your last bottle of wine before slipping out the back door with your boyfriend. I was one sick puppy. The truth is after the first drink, I never knew what was going to happen.

People often ask me how I left my hometown in California for the East coast, sight unseen. I tell them I did not leave, I fled. I had so overstayed my welcome. Like a dog that had marked every place with pee, I had run out of spots to mark and my whole world was smelly. I needed a fresh start, a geographic do-over.

I had been living in the D.C. area for almost seven months when I hit my alcohol and bulimia bottom. Although I had vowed not to drink when I moved from my hometown to Washington in mid-June that year, I was drunk as a skunk on the Capitol Mall when the Beach Boys were bringing in the 4th of July for millions with a free concert. My "promise" to myself was to stop drinking and to stop being bulimic on this new adventure across the country, but I was unable to keep either one of those commitments for more than 30 days. I had a chronic problem of letting myself down.

My weekends were marked by drinking binges starting at Happy

Hour on Thursday with friends from the office. I would have to stay the night with them because after a couple of White Russians or a glass or two of wine, I couldn't remember how to get home. I ended up in really compromising situations where I was forced to stay places and do things that I never would have done sober. I would then get home the next day and "party" at my apartment with friends, neighbors and my roommate. I usually didn't venture far from home on Saturdays due to the humiliating adventure of the previous night when I could not get home. But I would stay up very late until the booze ran out, making phone calls back to the West Coast to talk to old boyfriends and friends and beg them to come and see me. At the age of 23, I was a twisted and pathetic drunk.

On Sundays I would be sick, really sick, nauseous and shaky the whole day. Mondays, I would still be sick and I would get dressed for work and walk to the Metro with a barf bag in case I vomited. The ride into Dupont Circle was fraught with bumps and nausea intermittently so I would be sick to my stomach for the entire ride. Then I would get out of the subway and measure my path to my office from one garbage can to the next, in case I had to hurl. I did hurl occasionally and I felt disgusted at what I had become. Yet, that did not signal to me that I had a problem.

By Wednesdays, I would feel better. No more nausea and sea-sickness on the Metro. By Thursdays, I would go out again and be careful to have "just one" beer on the way home from work. I would have forgotten already about how sick and disgusted I was earlier in the week and I would do it all again, starting at Happy Hour with officemates, and so on and so on, endlessly, every weekend.

Late one night while I was living in Washington, I phoned the Alcoholics Anonymous hotline. I really don't know why. I just did. I asked for the nearest meeting to Capitol Hill. I was done. I had just finished a bucket of chicken and had drunk four super sweet wine coolers. I was sick as a dog and I was tired of getting drunk all alone and throwing up.

It was a Thursday evening. I had started the party early before arriving home and got my stash for the night: Popeye's and wine coolers. Nine days earlier, I had turned 24. For some reason, that night I hit my bottom. It was not spectacular. I just had that moment of clarity where I knew that I did not want to live that way anymore. I had become my father. In spite of my vow not to become a weekend drunk like him, I was.

I called AA. There was a meeting the next day in the basement of the Senate building. Even in that alcoholic stupor, I thought, "No way, politicians don't get sober. How do they do business if they can't drink?"

I attended both out of curiosity and desperation. I do not remember much about that meeting. I remember seeing very powerful men and women in suits admitting that they were alcoholics and that their lives were better now that they were not drinking. No one "looked" like an alcoholic. I got a meeting schedule and I went to another meeting in Georgetown that same day after work. That meeting was to become my home group. For the next six months, I went to meetings at the Westside Club up to three times a day on the weekends. I was home.

My second meeting was the one that I can recall most clearly. It was upstairs above some shops on Wisconsin Avenue in Georgetown. I walked in and I felt like I was "on base" during a game of tag. The truth is that for my whole life I had felt like I was running and trying not to get tagged. I was always looking for the safe zone.

The meeting room was dark and musty. People were smoking and drinking coffee. An older man came up to me and offered to be my sponsor. Then a couple of women approached me and told me to stay away from the old man and that they would find me a female sponsor. I took them up on their offer. I would have done anything at that moment to feel the relief from the shame and guilt that I had been carrying around for the last decade.

I heard the term "Surrender to Win" at my first meeting at the Westside Club. I thought that was the most ingenious phrase I had ever heard. I heard that it was the first drink that got me drunk, not the second or third. "Oh," I thought to myself. "I get it!"

I really did think it was the second or third drink and I had been trying for years to stop after one. One drink gave me that lightheaded buzz and the warmth of indescribable love for all of mankind, I just thought the second one would sustain that feeling, not make me a stumbling drunk. But, that strategy NEVER worked.

Slowly, I got better and better and better. I remember thinking that all I had to do was stop drinking alcohol. When I said that out loud during a meeting, everyone chuckled.

I did not realize that, by making that choice to stay in the rooms of Alcoholics Anonymous, I had actually taken that first step to changing everything about my life. I have not ever gone back to the bottle after that first meeting on Capitol Hill. It is not to say that I was struck perfect overnight. However, I was able to admit that I was powerless, that my life sucked and I wanted something different. Different is exactly what I got. I got the 12 Steps.

CHAPTER 4

. . . .

The Bumpy Road

We admitted that we are powerless over alcohol
and that our lives had become unmanageable.
—STEP ONE FROM THE 12-STEP PROGRAM
OF ALCOHOLICS ANONYMOUS

For the first six months, I was on a predictable pink cloud. I was so happy to have escaped the gates of hell that everything was wonderful. It *was* wonderful. I worked and went to meetings. I told my roommate that I was an alcoholic and she disagreed with me. She told me I was overreacting. She said that she drank as often as I did and she wasn't an alcoholic!

Good thing I did not buy that one. I was told that it did not matter how much I drank or how often I drank, what mattered was how it made me feel. And it made me feel rotten inside. After the first six months I had built a solid network of clean and sober friends. I had experienced a sober dance, water skiing sober, baseball games, camping, movies, long car trips and concerts—all sober. I was beginning to think I could do it. And then I moved to another state to start law school.

I went to law school in a cold Eastern state. As I already mentioned, I am from California. I had seen snow a couple of times when I drove to it. I am not only from California, born and raised, but I am FROM California, 8th generation. My DNA is California DNA, which means I hate to be cold. I had never lived in snow.

I chose a chilly East Coast school because I needed to stay indoors and study. I knew myself well enough to know that I could not go to law school in a big exciting city or a beach town, because then I would not be able to impose the discipline necessary to study. So I chose my law school on that basis (and they also gave me some money which I would have been a fool to pass up).

At six months sober, I still associated snow with hot buttered rum and peppermint Schnapps. I suspect my sponsor was onto me, since she called ahead and had people from the "fellowship" meet me at the airport. She said that she did not want me to forget who I really was, so people would be at the other end to take me to a meeting as soon as I arrived.

They say that when you walk into the rooms of Alcoholics Anonymous, a cloak of love is put around you that you can never shake, so you might as well stay. I have also heard it said that once you go to an AA meeting, it screws up the party forever. Nevertheless, Tom picked me up at the airport, took me to my dorm and let me unpack and then proceeded to take me to a meeting.

I LOVED Tom. He was beautiful. As is common with newly sober, desperate and needy alcoholic men and women, I was all about the pair of pants (boys) at that stage of my sobriety and I really had the time of my life with lots of dating. Sober dating of course, nevertheless dating.

I had no boundaries at this time and everyone was fair game. I am sure they saw me coming from a mile away. I tended to attract other needy newly recovered souls. It was never a match made in heaven and I quickly learned that sex was empty, just like drinking.

Roger, an elderly AA member who drove a soft-top green Belvedere, was another character who came into my life in those first few weeks at law school.

My roommate was very curious that I had so many "friends"

in upstate New York, as I was a Mexican from California who had previously never left the zip code. And why would I have an old man for a friend? It was stressful, so I told her he was my uncle. After that I called him Uncle Roger. It was delightful in a twisted way. He would drive up in his really outrageous Belvedere and honk his horn and she would announce that my "uncle" was here. I would secretly giggle.

What is apparent in hindsight is that I was so new and not yet well. I was a fresh one. Fresh into recovery and not any clue how to do life without a drink. After Tom picked me up from the airport and got me well connected to the AA clubhouse, I got a new sponsor and right away, I began to go to daily meetings. I actually believed back then that I had to attend at least one meeting a day or I might drink again.

I was very nervous on my first day of law school. I was overwhelmed by the majesty of the campus itself. It had an old Ivy League type of greatness with its large brick buildings with ivy and other beautiful greenery climbing the fences throughout the campus. Moreover, the law school building was on the top of a hill that looked down over the rest of the campus. It was love at first sight. Basically, back then I had really raw emotions and I felt deep love or deep fear about everything and everyone around me.

So I arrived at the law school for a pre-school year summer session for kids like me who had barely made it in. I was one of 30 or so students from diverse backgrounds who were afforded an opportunity to succeed. It was a phenomenal opportunity, but I was frazzled and terrified of making a mistake.

At my first class, the teacher sat us in a circle and asked each of us in turn to say a little bit about ourselves. I could not hear what other people were saying because I was struck with a fear that only another alcoholic could understand. By that time I had stated the phrase "I am Eleanor and I am an alcoholic" at least 200 times, so I was afraid that when it came to be my turn to introduce myself that I would revert to my AA experience and say "Hi, I am Eleanor and I am an alcoholic." I was concentrating really hard on not saying that phrase.

Luckily, when my turn came, I was able to divert myself from that phrase successfully. I told them my name but I did not say I was an alcoholic. But, what happened next was equally embarrassing and I am sure caused a bit of concern. I had gotten through the gauntlet and the moment of terror passed, only for me to totally screw up by saying "Hello!" out loud to the next person as though I was in an AA meeting!

He introduced himself as "Charlie" and I said really loud to him (and of course no one else said anything), "Hi, Charlie!"

After I said it, I realized what I had done in this very serious place where I was speaking out of turn. Charlie looked right at me and smiled and said "Hi" back to me directly. After that, Charlie thought I liked him. I did like him, but not in that way. So I spent quite a bit of time dodging romantic vibes from him for months.

In law school, I was so not in my element. It was all so foreign to me. I drank my way through high school and college, so I did not even know what I was capable of learning and I certainly had no idea about how to study. I was building the bridge as I was crossing it and I did not know what else to do but go to meetings and not drink, "one day at a time" as we say in AA. It seems to work for the most part.

I joined study groups and founded the university's first Latino law school organization. I was one of two ethnic Mexican-Americans at the school. The other student was a young man from Los Angeles and he was wonderful. The other Latinos were mostly Puerto Rican and Cuban. For the most part, we partied (no alcohol for me), cooked and studied together with all the other diverse kids as well.

There was an AA meeting every day at noon on campus, so I made fast friends with older law students who were also recovering alcoholics. They helped me a lot. They gave me good advice and old outlines for the classes that I was taking. They met me at meetings and we ate lunch together and just tried to do the next right thing.

I got my first paying legal job from a member of Alcoholics Anonymous. He owned a bankruptcy law firm and he paid me to clerk for him. Mostly, I looked up liens in the county recorder's office for him. It was wonderful. After the late summer dorm living, I rented a room in a house full of AA women. Everybody from the AA group took care of me and loved me. They gave me a hard time when I needed it, but mostly they loved me and, for the first time in my life, I felt I was loved and had all my needs met.

My first semester exams were scary. I studied ALL THE TIME. I had never in my life studied like I did in law school. We had what are called "sudden death" finals because there is only one final per semester and if you failed, you failed. If you failed a class, you had to take it over again. There was no chance to do a paper or take another exam to get to a passing grade.

I was very nervous for my first set of exams. In my mind, disaster was looming. I studied all night for Civil Procedure, my most challenging class, even though I had studied plenty the weeks and months before. I thought if I could just study more, surely I would do better. The "more is better" lie got me again.

Instead, what happened is that I went to the exam most likely with no food and with no sleep and I had a hypoglycemic attack! I got very lightheaded and I could not see the words on the paper. The words blurred together and I was nauseous. I am not sure what I wrote down, if anything. I remember thinking that I had to get out of there before I passed out. Now I probably would have gone to the professor and explained my physical illness, but I had no idea that that might have helped me get an opportunity to take the test again. Instead I failed the exam and I had to take Civil Procedure as a 2L (second year law student), which turned out to be okay. I passed it easily and, of course, did eventually graduate from law school.

I have never pulled another all-nighter since then. I will not even take a red-eye if I can help it because I so desperately need my sleep in order to function. I pulled all-nighters all the time in college when I was drinking and smoking, but I had never had the type of reaction that plagued that first law school exam. It was a really hard lesson to learn to take care of myself and to have faith that enough is enough when it comes to studying or anything else, as I was slowly beginning to discover. I talked about it a lot at my meetings and they told me to be quiet and count my blessings, so I did.

It was always cold in that upstate city. I always felt like an unmade bed. My peers were from wealthy families whose parents had been to law school or were medical doctors. I was from a Mexican family in Northern California with one parent whose family was from Mexico and one parent whose family had been in California for seven generations but still spoke Spanish and ate beans and rice: the original Californios.

I was used to California's warmth, the sun and having lots of people around that looked like me. My peers showed up at school in fur coats, driven to the door by limo drivers. I walked a couple of miles each day in the snowy weather with at least 10 pounds of books on my back. They wore designer clothes and beautiful jewelry and I wore fake London Fog trench coats and icicles were stuck to my nose when I finally hauled myself up the hill to the law school's grand entrance.

I thought it wasn't fair. I could not even wear jewelry because it was so cold that the earrings would freeze and burn my ears and neck if they touched my skin. In every way, I was just barely managing to get by. Newly sober, poor as dirt, no one in my family to tell me what classes to take or what internships to apply for and no one in my family nearby to give me a hug or a cup of coffee.

I called home frequently in those days because I am pretty sure I suffered from what today would probably be diagnosed as anxiety. I probably could have used meds, but instead I drank lots of coffee and smoked cigarettes.

One day as I was standing at the ATM machine, I could not remember my PIN number. I really needed to remember the number but I simply couldn't access the memory.

I was devastated. I thought about throwing in the towel, but when I called home to cry and asked permission to come home, the answer was always the same: No. My mother told me to stay there and finish what I started. She told me to go to a meeting and ask for help. So I did.

I also went to a therapist at the law school because of the anxiety. I felt an immense pressure to succeed and it seemed as though I was flying without a net. In truth, I *was* flying without a net. I was in completely foreign territory. I did not have my family or my booze. What in the world was I thinking, starting law school like this?

The therapist pointed out that I was sabotaging myself with the anxiety, which caused me to forget my PIN number. Similarly, I set myself up with the all-nighter that caused me to fail my test. She urged me to explore why I was not taking better care of myself and asked me to trust that I hadn't come this far to fail.

I do not recall how long I continued in therapy, but I do recall the relief I felt knowing that I was not an enigma and that I would grow out of the anxiety if I would begin to have some faith in things greater than myself. Hmmmm. Where had I heard that before?

In those early days, I whined a lot at meetings. I found plenty of meetings and I still attended daily. The Old Timers told me lawyers couldn't stay sober and they asked me why I was going to law school. After I failed my first year Civil Procedure class, my unsympathetic AA friends told me I was lucky I had the brain cells to retake the class and to shut the hell up. I never got sympathy from them, although they did spot me a couple of dollars here and there when I whined I could not afford hair spray and that hair spray was really my only luxury in life.

Then I met Todd. Todd was the love of my life for the next three years. People in recovery are advised to avoid making any major life changes in the first year of recovery; however I had moved to a new state, started law school and then moved in with my first sober boyfriend within the first eight months. I never listened well.

Fortunately, Todd took really good care of me. He was a snowplow driver for the state. To me, he looked like a Greek God. He was built like an Adonis and his blue eyes were deep pools of mystery. It really was love at first sight. He was newly sober too, of course.

Todd and I lived together for the next three years. I was spoiled by his unconditional love for me. He taught me lessons of selflessness and loyalty that I had never known. He followed me back to California at the end of my second year of law school when I decided to finish my last year as a non-matriculated law student at a local university. We grew apart as I got closer to launching into my legal career.

Leaving him was the second hardest thing that had ever happened in my life. The first was when my father got sick. Todd had been my angel. He saved me from the distress of navigating life alone without booze in those first two years of law school. He was my precursor to letting people in, although ironically, I never really let Todd in. He was as new and dysfunctional as I was, so we made a good pair for a while.

My first summer in law school, I clerked for an equal rights advocate, a former president of the National Organization for Women. I found her work to be exciting and meaningful. She had a home office, so I did everything for her from legal research to fetching firewood. I loved her and I wanted to be like her.

My second year at law school went much more smoothly than the first. I did not fail any classes and I slept before exams. Todd and I had a lovely apartment and he drove me everywhere, so no more trudging miles and miles in the snow up the hill with 10 pounds of books in my pack.

He was a godsend. We cooked scrapple for dinner because all our money went to rent and gas. We had a lovely life in spite of being two very dysfunctional newly sober humans.

I made him sign a contract not to leave me if I agreed to move in with him. That is how insecure I was. We agreed that we'd wait 30 days if we were mad at one another before we made a decision to abandon the relationship. We both signed it. I was trying to form a contract with him to protect myself from being hurt.

After my second year of law school, I went to another large city to work for the Federal government. I lived with my aunt in a nearby town that summer and took a daily hour-long bus trip into the center of the city.

Coincidently, there was a man who got on the bus each morning a couple of stops after me. He was always wearing a business suit and at first glance, he seemed quite dapper. Then he would secretly pull out a bottle of hard liquor from a brown bag and nurse it the whole way into the city. It smelled sickly sweet and pungent; it was definitely alcohol. Since I was clean and sober, I could smell alcohol a mile away. He would drink and doze, drink and doze. I never saw him get off. And I never saw him at the end of the day. But I always saw him again the next morning: same look, same bag, same routine . . . drink and doze, drink and doze. I wondered if he even had a job. I imagined him riding the bus all day, lying to his wife and telling her that he was going to work. I wondered what would happen when she found out. I wondered if he had children and if they knew their father was very, very ill.

He made me want to stay clean and sober. I never thought to share the 12 Steps with him. I think that I felt too new and too scared. I did not really want him to get to know me. He was my dark angel. He was someone God was showing me so that I could see my possible future. I went to meetings every day at noon. I found a meeting each day of the week in the city so that I could maintain my meeting a day, maintain the winning formula and never end up like the man on the bus.

I look back now and realize this was when I truly began to recover. I had it so easy at school with my clean and sober life and friends. Living in this city for the summer and seeing my possible future without AA right there on the bus each morning was a grim awakening. I saw clearly that I had work to do if I was going to stay sober.

I went to a nearby state university for my third year of law school in order to better prepare myself for the California bar exam. Todd moved with me.

I had a great year. I worked for a state agency that focused on access and fairness. I met great friends. I was also near my family and went to meetings every day with people that I had known all my life. I went to meetings with my father, my brother, my sister, my cousins and long-time family friends. It was a good time.

I met a recruiter at the law school job fair, someone I would work with in the future years. Towards the end of the second semester of my third year, I got an interview for a very interesting job.

I asked my father to drive me to the interview, feeling he was my good luck charm. It seemed that if Dad were along, everything would work out. When he was clean and sober he was a lightening rod for success. He drove me to the interview and waited outside for me. After the interview, as he was driving me home, I had a feeling of complete certainty that I had the job. Sure enough, I did get it. My talisman worked again.

Soon after that, I was to leave my family and friends again for a new journey. I was so ready to start my new life as a law clerk in a big city.

I was 27 when my father got sick. It was the worst time of my life. I was lost, beside myself and did not know how I was going to proceed on the planet with him gone. Luckily for me, but not so lucky for him, it took him three long years to die.

Dad was diagnosed with stomach cancer in the summer of 1989 on the day before I was scheduled to take the California bar exam. I remember the exact moment that we were told. I was at my family home even though I had my own apartment up the street.

My mother's tile floors kept it cool inside despite the heat outside. That part of California has dry heat, the kind you can tolerate because you don't start sweating the moment you step outside. It's the kind of heat that heats up the sidewalks but kids walk on them anyway with bare feet because it is summer and that is what kids do in the summer. Kids walk barefoot and have Kool-aid sales.

Dad had been experiencing stomach pain for months, he thought from stomach ulcers. He continued to pressure his doctor for relief as the pain intensified, but he never complained. My father never missed a day of work, I'm sure out of pride for his ascension from laborer to corporate executive. I can remember his fortitude, even after they had taken many of his organs and his weight had dwindled to half of what it should have been. He was a faithful employee from my earliest memories. Even if he had been drunk all weekend, thrown in jail or kicked out of a bar, he still always made it to work as far as I could tell.

In fact, we never went on vacation as a family. My mother would ask why in the world we would go camping like other families when she had grown up in migrant camps along with other farm workers. Our family worked. We did not go on vacation or believe in leisure. Now I realize that both my parents had to work at low paying jobs to pay the bills. In those days, it is highly likely that time away from work meant there would be no money coming in.

That day in June of 1989, my father had gone to the doctor for an internal stomach probe so that the doctor could see just how bad the ulcers were. What they found was that my father's stomach was one big tumor. It was stomach cancer. The prognosis was terminal.

I was shocked. Time stood still. My father, my big strong hero who never showed any emotion except excitement over his children and grandchildren, was crumpled into a weeping and disbelieving human before my eyes. The cancer had taken away his hero status in a swift second and it would snatch him from us at the age of 48. I did not want to believe my ears. For many months after that fateful day, a part of me did not believe that my father would actually die.

I was three years sober the day I heard the news of my father's impending death. I told Dad that I would probably have to drink. He looked at me, a man that had just been given a death sentence, who was himself fifteen years clean and sober at that time, and told me that he was not going to drink. So I thought to myself, "If he is not going to drink, then surely I should not. After all, it really isn't all about me, or is it?"

I told Dad that I would be unable to take the California bar exam the following day. I was simply too devastated by the news of his cancer. He pleaded with me to take the exam. "Pleaded" is an overstatement. He asked me once to take it, but you see, my father rarely asked me for anything, so to me it seemed that it was a plea.

I took the exam the next day. The morning of the exam, I arose numb and disbelieving still. I dressed in one of his sweaters for good luck and I went to my test. I flunked it by 11 points. Needless to say, I did pass it on the second try, no problem (with the same sweater—lime green cardigan—the kind the golfers wear although my father never golfed).

Shortly after I took the bar exam, I left for my new job without Todd. I told him that he could not follow me around any longer, but that I still wanted to be "good friends."

I had never really lived alone. I had lived at home and then with a series of roommates. Now I was headed to a new city and a new life to live alone in an apartment. After three years together and even though I was the one who broke off our relationship, without Todd, I felt that I left a limb behind. I was headed for a new adventure. I had mixed feelings of excitement and sadness.

I moved two hours away to start my first legal job in a large metropolitan Bay Area city. Todd met his new wife and I met my future husband in short order. They say that people are in our lives for reasons and for seasons. He was definitely in my life at the perfect time and we loved one another honestly and purely. I let him go with love, but he left a footprint on my heart that will be there for all time.

I arrived in my new city with my law degree and a job. At that point, I did not know if I had passed my first bar exam. I had secured a paying law clerkship, a feat virtually unheard of in the public sector.

I stayed with my cousin and his wife until I got my first paycheck. They were a very thoughtful couple who took me in and made me feel quite welcome. I found my 12-Step meetings immediately, having taken a lesson from my first sponsor. I resumed my daily attendance just as I had done for the prior three years. At the time, I understood that attending at least one meeting a day was critical to my sobriety.

I found a one-bedroom apartment and with my first pay check, put down a deposit, paid the first and last month's rent and moved in. I had no furniture and slept on the floor. With the next paycheck I bought a bed on time from Levitz Furniture Store. I still have that bed today. It was a really nice bed, but it was also a symbol that I had grown up. I wasn't depending on anyone anymore. I was self-sufficient.

This was something I had yearned to be for my entire life, especially after seeing my mother struggle throughout my childhood with a serious lack of any independence, physical, emotional or otherwise. For me, there would be no more father, Todd or family "helping." I did it! (I didn't realize at the time that Higher Power did it.)

Within six months, I met Mike, the man who was to become my husband. We were both volunteering for a local organization that served underprivileged youth. When we met, I was dating someone else, but I knew that man was not for me. I knew that it was a fling and probably more like a rebound relationship after Todd. So when I first met Mike, I was intrigued. He was nothing like the other men I had dated all my life. He was normal and had nothing discernibly wrong with him.

I do not know if I ever trusted love. Even after I had an engagement ring on my finger, I kept thinking Mike would leave at any minute. It was really hard for me to believe that such a normal person would love such a damaged person. Being with Mike was a mirror for me, a mirror that showed me everything I was not. His parents planned him. They could afford him. His father went to Cornell University and his mother was a stay-at-home mom who played tennis, baked pies and loved him up as much as she possibly could.

We could not have come from more different backgrounds. I kept thinking that if he understood who I really was that he would never want to marry me. So, I kept telling him the downside: "You know I am an alcoholic? You know that my parents didn't plan me and we collected food stamps? You know I was abused as a child?" And so on. I kept thinking that if he heard the right question he would realize that he made a horrible mistake.

As hard as I tried, I couldn't shake him. After I brought him home to meet my family, my sisters took me aside and told me not to blow it. They thought he was wonderful. Twenty years later, they still do.

My friends in AA told me to keep dating him even though I told them he was different and I wasn't sure if I liked him. He had no exciting dark side. My AA sponsor told me to keep dating him and to stop dating everyone else. Everyone seemed to know me better than I knew myself in those days.

Eventually, I decided that if I couldn't get Mike to wake up to the reality of my damaged persona, I'd take the initiative and tell his family. Surely, they would tell Mike that he was crazy to stay with someone like me. I told Mike that I was going to inform his mother that I am a recovering alcoholic. He told me to go ahead and "break" the news. Mike did not seem to understand the gravity of the situation. In those days, for me everything was high drama. I figured out I might as well end things sooner rather than later.

So we went to his family's home about an hour away from the

city we lived in at that time. I was sitting at the dining room table with a cup of tea and my future mother-in-law. I told her that I had something to say to her. She sat down and gave me her full attention. I was sure that she would never expect what was to come next; she was probably expecting me to say I was pregnant.

"I am a recovering alcoholic," I blurted out.

I tried to read her face. It was still full of kindness and compassion as it always was. After I was finished, she told me that she loved me *more*! So my master plan to shake the man I loved and his family failed, in spite of my best efforts at self-sabotage. I realized I might as well just let them love me. This was all new territory for me, to be sure.

Mike and I had a beautiful wedding. My very ill father was able to walk me down the aisle. I will cherish that moment forever. He was so proud and so was I. More than 300 people gathered to celebrate our public commitment to one another. The church was packed with our families. Exquisitely costumed mariachis played for the wedding and then paraded us the three blocks through a park to our reception hall. The sun was shining and lots of people were out and about to see the show. I felt like a princess in my white beaded and lacey dress with the enormously long train carried by all my beautiful bridesmaids. For that moment, with five years of sobriety, I felt healed.

After the wedding, while we were still fresh from taking our vows my father took Mike and me aside. He was very ill and in a great deal of pain. He actually had to go home to rest between the wedding and the reception. He gave us his words of wisdom: "Do the opposite of what we did." Those were Dad's guiding words.

When Mike and I left the reception that night, I felt like Cinderella in her horse drawn carriage with my Prince Charming, stepping into a limousine and being driven to the Saint Francis Hotel in San Francisco where his parents had spent their honeymoon night.

I had gotten fake nails for the wedding. On that evening, I broke a nail while I was moving luggage. It was so painful that I needed

Tylenol and ice packs sent up from the front desk. Mishaps aside, it was a wonderful few days. Mike and I returned to the Saint Francis for years to celebrate our anniversary.

The first year of our marriage was hard because I was still so afraid that it wasn't real. I am not sure how someone as unworthy as I could land a mate like Mike. He lived to make me happy. He often put his own wellbeing aside so that I could have my needs met. We drove back and forth to my hometown as often as twice a week to see my dying Father. He was so good to me and so loving.

I ended up back in counseling at the local community center specializing in death and dying to try to ward off the grief that I felt around my father's impending death. By the time he died, I was ready. I was afraid we might have unfinished business. I looked for father/daughter books and I couldn't find any that talked about loving relationships between fathers and their daughters, only books that were written about dysfunctional relationships. I was so committed to healing with my father before his death that I am sure I taxed his last days with my exploration and prying to make sure we were "okay."

I recall spending the night at the house during those last weeks with my father. Everyone knew this was a death vigil. Mike would drive me in. Mike would get food for everyone. We would make sure that there was plenty to eat for everyone. Then he would leave me to my grief and sadness with my sisters and my brother. I recall seeing the women take care of my father. My Aunt Kelly, my Aunt Lorraine and my mother would gather around his bed and make sure that he was clean and comfortable.

In those moments, I was so proud to be 8th generation Californio on my mother's side. I remember feeling like I belonged to something so much bigger than myself. I would take my turn reading him prayers over and over again. We did not leave his side for weeks. Each one of us would tell him it was okay for him to pass. Then we would do our best to help him. The process of dying can be long, painful and difficult.

He told me that he was not afraid of dying. He was only very sad to be leaving all the people that he loved. At the end, I know that he wanted to die because it was just too painful to live. The cancer took him. The cancer ate away at his beautiful biceps and his huge thighs. He was no more the man that he had been.

I thought that when my father died, I would no longer have the structure or motivation to move forward with the self-discipline and self-respect that my father demanded of me. I was afraid that I would default into my base desires for alcohol, food and sex without discrimination. I was wondering how I would ever integrate his morals and expectations to my inner being. I am happy to say it all happened easily and without effort. As petrified as I was about "going wild" without my dad, my ballast, it did not happen.

After my father passed, I realized that he was with me always. My good luck charm was inside of me. I had him with me 100% of the time now to watch over me and to guide me. I convinced myself that God had taken Dad to watch over abused and neglected children.

I was then working as a government attorney and was just beginning to work in the field of child maltreatment and criminal justice. I told myself that Dad was now going to be a guardian angel to many children now that he had successfully raised his own.

My babies came and my marriage weathered much those years when I was still eating addictively. Many of those years are a blur. I was trying to climb the law firm ladder and be a mom and wife all at the same time.

As idyllic as my life might seem to others, I was still riddled with fear, doubt and insecurity. The more I tried to control things, the unhappier and fatter I got. I had two beautiful girls. One came with an old soul and the other with the trickster heart who has always made all of us so happy to be alive. Each has her own sets of gifts and it makes me feel better just to be around them.

Dad never met my two wonder girls, but I always knew that he was close. When the oldest had any problems, I would tell her to talk to her grandfather who now lived with the man on the moon. I would gaze out the window with her and point at the moon and show her the eyes and nose shapes that were visible to me and I would tell her that Grandpa was up there. She believed me and we often spoke of Grandpa who lived with the man on the moon.

Mike and I had our first child almost two years after we were married. Mary came to us with all her wisdom already placed in her soul. She is one of my greatest teachers, after my father. Mary was born with a mission and a vision about the world and it was all good. In her early baby years, I threatened to leave Mike a few times because I was exhausted all the time and I was fat. I am really glad I didn't.

One day, I packed my little car and put Mary in the back seat and told Mike that I was going home to my mother. He sat in the passenger seat and wouldn't get out. I am really glad he wouldn't get out. He said Mary was half his. I said no, she was not. I conceived her, carried her and now I was her sole food supply. I asked which part of her was his. I know I must have looked like a woman crazed, but he just sat there loving me from a distance until it seemed hours passed and I had to go to the bathroom. A battle of the wills and the bladder won out. I stayed.

Partners should be trained to sit in the car the way Mike did. I wanted him to stay, I just couldn't say it. I wanted him to love me and my new baby, I just couldn't say it. I was stuck at four years old and I was throwing a major tantrum. I just wanted to be safe and cared for and that is what he did. He gave me a beautiful, chaos-free home and he loved me. He never left.

My second child was born a few years later. Claire came out full of dimples and trickery. She showed me that the spirit is much bigger than the body. From the start, she permeated every room she entered even when she was brand new and only weighed seven pounds. She lit up my life and fueled my desire to make a happy, stable home.

It took years, but finally I have grown up. I learned that being in a relationship with a life partner is the most intense thing a human can do. I also learned that being a parent is the second most intense thing we do. No wonder I grew so much! I do trust today. My husband is my spiritual partner. He teaches me lessons about myself every day that have nothing to do with the material world. He and I are, in fact, soul mates. I am grateful for his infinite patience, his ability to see a part of me I didn't even know existed and to nurture me until I felt safe enough to reveal my true nature. I am so glad I surrendered and let him love me.

CHAPTER 5

● ■ ● ■ ● ■ ● ■ ● ■ ● ■ ●

Facing Food Addiction
in Sobriety

Major surrender number two took a really long time for me to get. I was fifteen years clean and sober when I hit my bottom with food. Many times over the years, I had surrendered certain foods, only to un-surrender them over and over again. I had come a long way, but I didn't really begin this second stage of healing until I faced my food addiction.

My first AA sponsor told me that I could not throw up anymore with my bulimia. She said that sober women don't throw up. So I stopped the bulimia the day I stopped drinking, 10 days after my 24th birthday.

I stopped throwing up, but I did not stop using food and having very serious body image obsession. After I got sober, my weight went down. I forgot to tell you that I was a fat bulimic. I always weighed about 185 pounds, even at the height of my bulimia, despite my 5'5" small-boned frame. I was huge. After I got sober, my weight dropped a bit and the puffiness of years of binging, purging and alcoholism went away, but I was still fat. I craved sugar, as is often the case with the newly sober alcoholics. I ate all the sugar I wanted. I was sober and felt that I needed to eat sugar in order to stay sober.

So over the first 15 years of my sobriety, I ate, starved, agonized and obsessed over my weight. My father's food addiction had been so severe that he killed himself with food in the last three years of his life. My father had gotten sober, but he never really addressed his addiction to food. He was an exercise bulimic. He would run five to ten miles a day during the week and eat very little. He would binge on the weekends on ice cream and junk protein like salami and chorizo. I never saw my father take a social bite, just like I never saw him take a social drink. He was either binging or restricting.

After Dad was diagnosed with stomach cancer and his stomach was removed, his doctor told him to eat only pureed foods to prolong his life. Dad would not or could not follow those directions. His food addiction was so overwhelming that he would eat steak in spite of the agony and pain he suffered to digest it with no stomach.

I knew that I had to do something about my twisted and perverse relationship with food. As the years wore on, it caused me marital discord, fear, doubt and insecurity and I knew inside that it would eventually kill me just like it killed my father.

At this point, I felt like nothing but a fraud despite my success professionally and as a mother. It is hard to describe the feeling of self-hatred I experienced when I ate something I knew would show up on my body in a matter of time, but I ate it anyway.

I was spending hours obsessing over what I was going to eat, when I was going to eat and then how I was going to still fit into this outfit or that outfit. It was a magnificent waste of time and energy and I knew it. My world was so small. All I wanted was to live as a great and noble human being and all I could think about was what I was going to eat and how much I hated my spouse. As a side note, my disease also manifested itself in self-hate and hatred for my very innocent husband.

It is said that addicts take hostages and that we are incapable of a true partnership with anyone. That really did apply to me. Everyone in my circle was a hostage to my disease and my demands. If they did not serve me in some way, I crossed them off the list and moved on.

There were times when I would ask Mike to go out and get some food item. I would have very specific instructions about that food item. He would dutifully go out to purchase it for me.

One night he went out for a burrito from my favorite Mexican Californian burrito place. He forgot to tell them to leave off the cheese (as I was a fat vegan at the time), and he brought it home to me like a servant who just wants to be appreciated. I took one bite, tasted the cheese and raged at him for not getting it right. I threw the burrito at him from across the kitchen and it landed on the floor making a royal mess. He quickly kneeled to salvage the meals sans the cheese. And he offered it back to me in a last desperate effort to make me happy. I rejected it and him as I often did around food events.

After the birth of my second child, I stayed fat. I was always fat actually, but I had lost some weight to get married. On my wedding day, I weighed 140 pounds and even that was too much on my frame. I am a petite woman with very small bones.

I went through life feeling old and dumpy. By the end of my eating nightmare, I felt like people were regarding me as my husband's dumpy mother when I was with him in public. Mike looks younger than he is and has a naturally lithe body. He is also very athletic and has a well-sculpted body from years of working out.

The better he looked, the crappier I felt. I was to become very familiar with rage during this period of my life. I had everything going for me. I had a beautiful husband who was hardworking, talented and from a solid family. I had two precious little girls. We traveled, vacationed and did whatever we wanted because of our huge two wage family income. Nevertheless, I was miserable.

On a trip to Hawaii at the depth of one of my cycles of self-hatred, I found Food Addicts in Recovery Anonymous (FA). I was so miserable in my own skin. At that time, I was a vegan who ate three meals a day with no snacking. I had many rules around food back then, rules that really only resulted in my being more and more miserable, bloated and fat. I scoured the island for locations where

I could get vegan style food three times a day. Imagine that in Hawaii!

I had no concept of planning ahead, so I did not think to go to a grocery store to cook for myself at our hotel where in fact we did have a kitchenette. At this point in my disease, food was all about the entertainment value. I could not wait to eat in order to escape, but then, after the food was gone, I was miserable because I was so fat.

So my day was a series of highs and lows around food intake and body image. I remember dragging my family from restaurant to restaurant in Hawaii to look at menus and determine if I could eat there. Sometimes my kids would want to stay at this restaurant or that restaurant, yet, like a Mad Hatter, I would still drag everyone out to keep looking for that perfect, yummy meal that was within my self-imposed and insane parameters.

I met Sophie on the beach at Waikiki early one morning in September of 2000. It was the 12-Step meeting, called the 12 Palms because there are 12 palm trees among which the meeting is nestled, providing a bit of privacy from the rest of the tourist-laden beach.

Sophie was a vision. She walked into the circle looking like a movie star in a simple black sundress, wearing a stunning black straw beach hat and sunglasses. I, on the other hand, felt like a beached whale. She was everything that I wanted to be: glamorous without effort, radiant and beautiful in a wholesome way. I did not want to speak with her because she was so clearly out of my league. We were at an AA meeting and she was there because that is what women in food recovery do when they travel, they go to AA meetings. I caught her attention when she overheard me commiserating with another fat and dumpy thirty-something about how fat I felt and that I wanted to join Jenny Craig.

Sophie offered to help. I wondered how in the world this perfect person could possibly help me! She said that I would have to give up flour and sugar. I told her that I could not imagine a planet without eating flour and sugar. She responded perfectly. She said that she bet that is how I felt when I gave up alcohol. Touché! She was right!

I was lost when I gave up alcohol and I remember finding my way, so I was willing to try it out. I had no idea what I was getting myself into. I was Svengalied. That is all I remember. I wanted to do whatever she told me. She was like the good witch of the North (although dressed in black). She had light radiating from her head like a halo. I believed in that moment on the beach with those kind eyes that she could save me. Sophie became my FA sponsor and for the next six months, I did exactly what she told me to do.

The first 90 days were sheer hell. I will not lie. I was so sad to lose my food. I was so angry to lose my best friend. I was devastated that Sophie had given me this simple solution because, in my mind, there was no going back. After AA, I knew better. I knew better, so I had to do better. I was also good for my word, so each day that I committed my food to her, I had to stick to it. I was too full of pride to leave the program and I was too full of pride to lie.

Now I know my stubbornness saved my life, but back then I was just really pissed off. It is a really good rule in FA that you cannot share at a meeting for the first 90 days. I would have only spewed poison. As we say in FA, I would have carried the mess and not the message. Miraculously after the first 90 days, on day 91 when I could share, I was beginning to be okay.

In those first few months, I was tired. Really tired. I was told that I was detoxing from the flour, sugar and the large quantities of food I was accustomed to consuming. I also gave up caffeine, so I was also detoxing from caffeine. There were entire weekends when I stayed on the couch, drifting in and out getting up only to eat my planned meals. I also felt like food was screaming at me during these first 90 days. I had severe cravings for foods that I had not eaten in years, like doughnuts and candy bars. I wanted to bathe in large buckets of chocolate and smear whipped cream all over my face. I was crazy.

Luckily, my car kept driving me to meetings even though I did not want to go. I wanted to go shopping. But my car, as though it had a mind of its own, kept driving me to meetings. I also kept eating as I had committed and after 90 days, I was thin and beautiful, like Sophie. I did not feel radiant yet, but I was thin! I had never in my wildest dreams thought I could weigh 120 pounds and wear a size four. I knew I would not have managed to get this body on my own, nor keep the weight off on my own.

After surrendering the food, the fog cleared. The minute I decided to follow someone else's plan for me around food, I felt tremendous and absolute relief. I woke up the 91st day feeling "clean" and hopeful. I had no real idea of what I had gotten myself into. They say that FA is like the mafia, once you're in, you can't get out. I had to call in and report every morsel of food for the next six months, every day of the week and speak to the 23-year-old who did not have kids or a husband and allow her to tell me about navigating life without taking the first bite. This was the accountability and the support I needed to get healthier even though I was kicking and screaming. It was a time of great confusion because I HATED FA and everyone in it, but I knew this was the solution and I kept going for my own good. It was not me that possessed me to follow directions: It truly was my higher self, breaking through core ego barriers and emotional walls of steel. I will forever love Sophie for putting up with me and saving my soul.

After being in FA for a few months, for the first time in my life, I came to believe that I am worthy of happiness too. If Sophie believed in me, why shouldn't I? I thought that God only helped good people. I was ruined for so many reasons. And besides, The Creator could not be bothered with such details as a woman who couldn't stop gluttony, lust and all the other traits of a broken spirit. Why would The Creator do that?

In recovery from food addiction, I learned that, in fact, I can be helped. I learned when I stopped eating and living addictively, I could actually love and serve humanity. No more hostage taking.

After surrendering the food, I learned that I am worth the journey and the work it takes to be whole. I surrendered in this final area of my life and I was willing to do whatever it took to experience the miracle of self-love. Clean and sober for 15 years, I embarked on the greatest internal journey of my life: to discover the source of all things.

The secret of abstinence and contented sobriety is to always put my new life first. I get up, say "thank you," read, pray, listen, prepare and pack my food, call my sponsor and take calls. My food is in order and silence is something that I seek and crave. I crave time alone with my Higher Power to access the genius of the Universe. This daily staging literally frees me up for a full day of love and service.

The rest follows. I have become a highly productive citizen because of FA. Due to the work that I have been willing to do, I currently have a healthy marriage, my parenting is helpful, not harmful, and I am a talented public servant.

When I was in my alcoholism and overeating disease, I wasted a great deal of time lamenting my awful marriage, my feelings of failure as a parent and my desire for more from my professional life. I was not acting in love and service because I was living in fear, doubt and insecurity.

If my program is in order, my reality and perception (which is 98% of life) is that my family is safe and well, my work is meaningful and satisfying, my marriage is happy and romantic and I am free to experience a joyful freedom from bondage.

I call this the essence of recovery. I have recovered my spirit or my authentic self. Because I learned to follow directions, I have been able with the help of my fellows and Higher Power, to break down the barriers that kept me from my higher self and stuck in ego. The development of certain disciplines has actually caused a tectonic plate shift in my consciousness that has led to a deeper understanding of life itself. In Richard Foster's book, *In Celebration of Discipline* this shift is described as follows:

"The purpose of discipline is freedom. Our aim is the freedom, not the discipline. The moment we make the discipline our central focus, we turn it into Law and lose the corresponding freedom."

Early on when I wanted to leave FA, I always focused on the discipline and not the freedom. Doing the tools takes discipline. Self-discipline gives me half a chance at recovery. *The Big Book* of AA promises that it is our birthright to be happy, joyous and free. But, I must sacrifice the excesses of my basic instincts for sex, security and status in order to have freedom.

I have learned that I have enough, I am enough and I do enough, so that I am no longer afraid as my animal brain would have me be. Due to the fact that I gave up what I perceived as the ultimate sacrifice—food in the form of flour, sugar and quantities—I have come to believe that there is enough of everything on the planet.

This is all a Disease of More, more, more. The AA guide *12 by 12* states in Step 4 that we have always wanted more than our fair share of everything. When I first started weighing and measuring, I really thought that the food portions I was allowed would not be enough. I was distressed and fearful. In those early days, it seemed that the hours between meals were the longest hours of my life. My sponsor had to reassure me that no one had ever starved to death between lunch and dinner! So I began to trust. I followed directions and I hung on to everyone else's success and the fact that there had been no reported deaths by starvation in my FA community.

When I couldn't stand the suffering of waiting between meals, I took naps. I now know that I was detoxing. I dreamt about food and eating things that I was no longer allowed to eat. My husband begged me to eat and said that only people who are starving have those types of dreams.

Little by little, I started living between meals. I had so much time now. I did not realize how much time I filled planning to eat, driving to eat, eating and then feeling bad about what I had eaten. I often ate until it was bedtime and just passed out.

After I put the food down, I had all this extra time. I started making jewelry. Here I was, working full-time at a high powered and demanding job, with two small daughters and a new program that took me out of the house three times a week for a an hour and a half meeting and I still had time to make jewelry.

People who come to FA are nearly always afraid that they don't have time for FA. But what we don't realize is the time suck of food addiction. The whole world opens up when we stop chasing the chow train. As it alludes to in the *Big Book,* in exchange for a fork and a knife, I have been given the keys to the kingdom.

Gradually I have come to know that I would get enough to eat and that I would survive on the portions allowed. Indeed, after I detoxed, I had more energy to live my life than I had ever had before. The aches and pains of being fat have left me and I am full of energy and vitality to live my full life. FA did not even require faith at first, because I had the burning bushes right in front of me. I did not have to believe in the program because I had the living examples in my presence at meetings three times per week. I saw their pictures! I was soon to join the ranks of the formerly obese, now thin, beautiful and recovered. What a miracle! I let myself be disciplined and now I am recovered.

Recovery has been a series of activities that have led me back to myself. Recovery has given me back to me. In return, I have been returned to God's service and now can benefit all of society. Now I actually do feel that I have enough of everything: love, money, companionship, material items, loyalty and trust. This is the miracle of the recovered. I gave up food pleasure for life pleasure.

● ● ● ● ● ● ● ● ● ● ● ● ●

CHAPTER 6

Coming into Being

Man may become the master of himself,
and of his environment because he has the power to
influence his own subconscious mind, and through it,
gain the cooperation of Infinite Intelligence.

—NAPOLEON HILL, *THINK AND GROW RICH*

How does one rise from a drunken, pitiful, groveling state of consciousness to live in the world with dignity and grace? How does the addict find freedom from addiction and craving? From years of experience, I can tell you confidently that it all centers in the mind. Having the gift of conscious thought has become the double-edged sword. The good news is that I was born with a brain and a higher intelligence than my animal friends. The bad news is that I was born with a brain and I have a tendency to believe everything it tells me. As an addict, my brain in its default mode tells me lies and tries to make sure that I am full of fear, doubt and insecurity. After obtaining this awareness, which could only occur after I stopped drinking and eating addictively, my life-long mission has been to change what I think. *? Change in Thinking*

Thank goodness for the 12 Steps and the 12 traditions of Alcoholics Anonymous that have given me explicit instructions on how to do just that: to change the way I think. Thank goodness for the

Recovery Movement. The Recovery Movement has given me wide berth and safe harbor over these many years. At first I thought that this was all a bunch of religious hocus-pocus.

What I have come to know is that it had nothing to do with religion and everything to do with me understanding that I am not in charge and that I am not God (should one exist).

At first, I did not know that I was actually changing the way I think. I thought I was just going to stop drinking and overeating. After years in recovery, however, I now realize that changing the way I think was exactly what Bill Wilson had in mind when he wrote the 12 Steps. He called it that "peculiar mental twist that precedes the first drink." Really ?!!???

It is the twisted thought that can kill: The drink before the drink or the bite before the bite. I have hung in there long enough to see that it is exactly my thinking that sets me up for failure and it is exactly my thinking that sets me up for success. Emerson said that the ancestor to every action is a thought. I had to change my thoughts. But first I needed to know how. How does someone *change her thoughts*? I found the solution in the 12 Steps. They are simple steps for complicated people.

I wrote this book to demonstrate that even the sickest among us can heal. Hope is here because I got better and so can you. This book is really about my experience with Step One: I admitted I was powerless over alcohol and my addiction to food—that my life had become unmanageable.

The main thing that I have learned is that life is a series of surrenders. It is not enough to surrender one time and "get it." The first step to problem solving is admitting that you have a problem. It has been said that we are incapable of admitting that we have a problem until we hit a bottom. But then new "problems" come and I can hit a new and different bottom before I know it.

I have been surrendering now for 25 years. I have surrendered alcohol, flour, sugar, quantities of food, chewing gum, other people, cigarettes, fantasizing, flirting, gossiping, diet soda, artificial sweeteners, true crime novels, worry and salt!

I am totally serious; I have had to give up all of these items in order to grow. In AA, we say, "You grow or you go." I have never been prepared to go anywhere else but right here. I was just trying to be "right here," in all the wrong ways. For all my faults, I always have been—and I am determined to be—in the present.

After years of self-examination, meditation and yes, even prayer (whatever that really is), I have emerged WHOLE. Feeling whole means no longer feeling as though I have a HOLE in the middle of my gut that can never be full enough; I walk today on sacred ground and live a sacred life. I have achieved wholesomeness.

It took time, tears and failure. It took painful realities and as though I gave birth to a whole new person, it took a team of people. I needed the midwife, the doctor, the anesthesiologist and the nurse. But alas, I am here and I am whole and it was hard, but it didn't kill me.

What I also know from the many 24 hours that I have put together, one day at a time, in recovery is that I can't stand, sit or lie still, or I will backslide. We addicts cannot rest on our laurels. So I am healed, but there is no "arriving:" I must keep on going forward or I will surely slip into old thinking and old behavior. So I strive daily to maintain the level of serenity that I have and to increase my understanding of what the universe would have me be and do.

CHAPTER 7

● ● ● ● ● ● ● ● ● ● ● ● ●

Surrendering to My Sponsor: Learning to Follow Directions

Isuffered from being a know-it-all. In fact, there should be a Know-It-Alls Anonymous. I caused myself so much misery with my closed mind and my absolute need to be right. So when I came into the 12 Steps and was told that I needed to get a sponsor and do what I was told, it was a foreign concept to me.

When you're in AA, your sponsor knows. Your sponsor knows the 12 spiritual tools and will not lead you astray. Picking the right sponsor is very important. Once you put the substances down, it is okay to trust your intuition on this. Find someone who has what you want and ask her how it was achieved. Pick someone with more than six months of recovery, preferably someone who has worked the steps and ideally someone with years of sobriety and abstinence. And then do what you are told. This is a simple instruction for complicated people. Believe me, I know.

And of course, women stay with the women and men stick with the men to avoid the obvious, and of course lesbians, gays and transgenders are welcome and choose sponsors accordingly.

In AA, I did what I was told because I did not want to drink again, and besides, they let me eat. I am dually addicted and I only had to give up one of the loves of my life in AA. I still smoked for the first year, I still ate sugar and flour and large quantities of food and I still ran around like a wild woman staying out late with few or no boundaries or discernment over boyfriends. It took a while, but, for the first time, I learned how to act right.

I remember the desperation of those days, no longer wanting to feel shame and guilt. The further I got away from the last drink, the less guilt I felt. I began to wake up with my head clear.

Early on, I recall seeing a rose in a garden as I walked to the Metro one day. It was so red and juicy, the morning hanging on that one perfect rose, leaving dewdrops that I could see and smell. I was overwhelmed with hope. The miracle of that moment is still with me all these years later.

In those days, if my sponsor told me that I had to stand on my hands in a corner and gargle peanut butter, I would have. It is called the Gift of Desperation (GOD). I had the gift without knowing that in fact, I had GOD. What surrender is really about is admitting that someone else knows more than you. Faith without works is dead.

So even though I had found a glimpse of a higher power at this point in the form of my sponsor, I had to make a decision to step out and do the next required task. I was ready. It is said that if you have one more rationalization left in you, you are not willing to go to any length to get help and live differently. I had no more moves, to be sure. So I did what I was told.

Compared to FA, AA is like having a sponsor light. My FA sponsor was all about my business. It makes sense. I did not have to weigh and measure my booze three times a day. In AA, I put the plug in the jug and the rest was open for discussion.

In FA, everything is open for discussion because if it isn't, it can lead me back to the addictive eating behavior. Each day I would spend 15 minutes first thing in the morning relating to my sponsor what I was going to eat, where, when and how I was going to eat and how things were going in my life. And this was usually at o'dark hundred. I think that I first was told to phone at 6 a.m. I did not previously even get out of bed until I absolutely had to. Big lifestyle changes were underway.

I was told not to engage in flirting or extra-marital activity of any sort.

I was told I could not put anything in my mouth without discussing it with her.

I was told that I was not to miss meetings under any circumstances. If I had to miss a meeting, I was to phone her ahead of time and seek "clearance."

I had to wake up at least 30 minutes before our call at 6 a.m. to do "quiet time" and then phone her every day on time and not a minute late.

For the first time in my life, I began to have discipline. I developed self-discipline: the kind that you want to have when no one is looking.

My sponsor made me take quiet time. She said that I had to spend 30 minutes in the morning showing up for my Higher Power. Before joining FA, I would roll out of bed 45 minutes before I had to be at work. I would shower, dress and leave the house. My husband and I had hired nannies to care for our children while we both worked long hours at very demanding jobs. I did not eat breakfast in those days and I did not take care of my own kids. I was living very far afield from my mothering, which was something that mattered most to me. When I was in my disease, I just didn't have time or energy for the children.

I was told to be up and ready to talk with my sponsor by 6 a.m. No rolling out of bed and tired voices on the phone. By 6, I was to have done my quiet time and prayed. All of this was monumental for me to accomplish. From that simple restructuring of my life, I was able to begin to eat breakfast and be with my kids before work. I started to be present in my own life.

After almost a decade, I am happy to report that I almost always awaken without an alarm before 5 each morning. I spend some time with my Higher Power in silence and contemplation. I'm a sponsor now, and I start taking my own calls from sponsees very early. I eat and prepare the breakfast for my family and myself, lunches, too, if necessary. I walk for a half an hour with my husband, call my sponsor and carpool kids to school, all before 8 a.m. This is a far cry from the woman who rolled out of bed at 7:15 to be at work by 8!

I feel so useful today. I feel so excited to tackle the day and to see what the Universe has in store for me. This is all because I surrendered my own idea of my life and how it was "supposed" to be.

The beauty of the 12 Steps is that we can do this at any time, at any age and at any stage of our lives. My first sponsor was 23 years old. My current sponsor is 72 years old. People come into the rooms of the 12 Steps at all ages. I feel fortunate to have started when I did.

In learning to put my food on the scale three times a day, I also learned to not only surrender to my addiction to that substance called food, but to the metaphor of life itself. I learned to do what I was told and to weigh and measure everything. I did all of this because I was willing to surrender to win.

More surrender while living life

I know how I got here. I know that I was conceived in a teen-age romance by my 19-year-old father and my 17-year-old mother soon after my brother was born. I also know that my soul had been here before, so there was no need for celebration of the physical birth. I had always known more, loved more and felt the grace of God long before I could name it.

As a four-year-old, I wanted to be a nun. I would walk around the house with a towel draped around my head like a nun's veil. In high school, I landed the role of Sister Sophia in *Sound of Music* and I actually got to wear a full nun's habit. Even though I no longer wanted to be a nun, I wanted to be good, so attaining the role was glorious!

I gave up the idea of being a nun early, because I felt bad and different soon after age four. I was unable to shake the feelings of "badness" for many years and I am not sure why I started to feel them or exactly when they left.

It is odd to say that I felt the Creator's grace and a sense of badness at the same time, but it is true. I suppose even the worst characters on the planet have glimpses of God's grace or they would probably end up killing themselves.

I was raised in a large extended Mexican-American family. I had uncles and aunts galore. The food and music were always abundant at family parties and on the weekends when we visited my grandparents about 10 miles down the road. I had plenty of people to love me. I had plenty of everything. Sadly though, and true to the addict mentality, I still felt that I did not belong and that I did not have enough.

It was not until after I became clean and sober and abstinent that I began a journey to become the person I was meant to be. All the research in life that I had done prior to January 24, 1986 was taking me further and further from my true self. As soon as I walked into the rooms of AA, I got back on track and I have been on that track ever since.

Becoming my authentic self has been an exciting, painful and rewarding journey. What a joy to have the opportunity to live this side of life! I am aware that many millions never get to a place of moving toward personhood for a variety of reasons. I feel grateful that I can get up every morning and start anew with grace and energy. I feel hopeful that as long as I give my one percent, doing my part but not feeling like I have to do more than my part, the universe will work with me to realize my wildest dreams, and then some. I am present.

CHAPTER 8

• • • • • • • • • • • • •

Early Lessons
in Surrender

The hallmark of the addict is the <u>inability to achieve staying power or consistency.</u> We tend to be really good at starting things and not so good at hanging in there and finishing things. They say it is not how you start, but it is how you finish that counts. The thing about life is that the finish is death, at least for this time around. It is easy to get tired and want to stop trying. It is also easy to say it is too hard and regress into old behavior patterns and slip into old thoughts.

<u>For the addict to stand still is to be in retrograde. If we stand still, we are really slipping backwards.</u> They say that recovery is like riding a unicycle and if you stop peddling, you fall off. We can't afford that. Each day we make progress, but it is only a fraction of what is needed. We have to give ten times the effort to gain one percent. That is where all the negative thinking and bad behavior took us. It is not enough for us to make progress and have a bad day here and there. <u>We have to be vigilant and constantly guard our recovery as the priceless treasure it is. Relapse is sneaky just like the disease.</u>

Developing discipline is remaining vigilant long after the desire has left you. <u>I can generally get a good start. I can do anything that excites me with its novelty and innovation.</u> But after the newness has worn off, I get bored and I rationalize that my newest discipline was never that great to begin with.

Here's a good example of my one-time lack of discipline. This has happened to me three times with joining a gym. The first time was in law school. As you may recall, it was very cold outside all the time in the city where I attended law school. I thought for sure that if I joined a gym, I would be compelled to attend the gym each day and work out, especially since there was a monthly fee and since I was a student, I did not have any money to waste. This worked for about a week. I went faithfully each day and worked out with the weight machines.

Then I stopped. I do not remember why I stopped or exactly when. I just remember that I stopped and never thought about it again, until I was trying to buy a house and discovered I had neglected to pay the last $300 gym fee and that had ruined my credit.

I had so completely forgotten about my commitment to go to the gym that I even stopped paying. I remember believing that if I moved 30 miles away, that the fee was no longer valid. I do not recall if I ever actually followed up on this belief and took care of whatever needed to be taken care of in order to stop the creditors from doing what they had to do to make me pay. I paid, of course, but as you can see, the denial was profound.

Then there was the second time that I joined a gym. In abstinence and sobriety, I agreed to a one-year contract to attend a gym near my office. I continued that time for a couple of months. I would go for the treadmill, the weights and the sauna. It did feel really great. At first I couldn't believe my lucky life. Get up, go to the gym, work out, steam room and then off to work. After about a month, I started to get lonely. I wanted company. I was leaving the house really early, so I was missing our family routine. I slowly started missing the gym workouts. I would tell myself that I would get back to it later. I never did. Each month when the bill came, my husband asked me if I was using the gym. Sometimes I lied and said "yes" because I was so mortified at the waste of money. I think

Peculiar mental Twist?

this was around the time that I stopped having my nails done just so I would balance out what I was spending on myself each month without too much guilt.

The third time I joined a gym, my whole family joined as a Christmas present to ourselves. My girls were not playing sports and we were worried that inactivity would lead to brain rot. Mike and the girls went for a while. I went with them one time, worked out for about 10 minutes and then hung out with them around the entrance waiting for Mike to be done. Then no one went with Mike. He kept going alone for several months and then he suspended our account. We can join anytime without paying a startup fee again. Somehow, I do not think I will be doing that unless I become unconscious again.

With exercise, I think if you chose something you love, you will continue it. I think that gyms are full of body-centered people who live shallow lives and I do not want to be around them. I do exercise, just not at the gym. Gyms are spiritually oppressive locations, like malls.

So there you are, an example of me not doing something after the "feel good" sensation wore off.

I must say that I believe the gym thing is not entirely typical of my life. I have been able to stick to things. They are usually around self-discipline and what I put into my body. External energy exertion and self-discipline are harder than eliminating things. I am able to walk for about a half an hour most days with my husband. I believe that if I exercise for 30 minutes five days a week that I am warding off heart disease and high blood pressure. This is not so hard for me to do and I do it even when I don't feel like it because my husband and the dog go with me. Mike and I just put on our tennis shoes and step out the door. It helps to have a partner to motivate me. It does not fit easily into my lifestyle, since I really have to fit my life around this half an hour, but I do it anyway because it is good for me. It requires discipline.

With my recovery program, sometimes the best I can do is not do something. I weigh and measure my food and I don't drink—one day at a time. I figure that the rest is bonus points. The staying power is that the days go by and the further I get from that last bite or the last drink, the clearer I get and the more restless my soul becomes to make a difference and to help someone. It is hard for me to help people when I feel fat or tired.

The beauty of these 12-Step programs is that by not eating and drinking one day at a time, my body has been returned to health and my head has been returned to right thinking. The staying power is almost automatic if I use the tools of the program and I act my way into right thinking. The tools that are given to us in FA are simple, but practical. There is a list of actions that I am to take each day, even when I do not want to.

The AA way is to bring the body and the mind will follow. We cannot think our way into right action, we have to act our way into right thinking. This is a basic tenet of recovery that is based on behavior modification. There is no way around it. I must do things I do not feel like doing in order to change.

I really can't help but grow if I keep doing what the program asks of me. It requires me to be honest, open and willing. It requires me to go to meetings and to make three outreach calls per day. It is hard to get lost in my own small world of petty grievances with all these people to talk to and all these places to go. At first, I felt pulled through the week. Sometimes I still do. The staying power is in the literal structure of the program. I bookend my day, my weeks and my months in this program. Prayer, reading, meditation in the morning and prayer, meditation and reading before bed. I am always aware of Higher Power because I am not eating or drinking.

Easy Does It, But Do It is one of the key phrases used in AA that keeps me in the game of life with an attitude of openness to the possibilities that present themselves. This reminds me that I have work to do, but that I should lighten up and take it easy. I cannot tell you how serious I was before I entered the recovery program. Everything was so serious; everything was a crisis or an event. I was so sensitive. I rarely laughed and I surely did not laugh at myself. Life was like quicksand and I was always trying to make my way out of it.

When I think of "Easy Does It," I think of my attitude and how I can change it if I want to change it.

Truthfully, a good attitude does not just come along all by itself. I have learned that I must cultivate it. William James, the noted philosopher, said it best: "The greatest discovery of our generation (1930s) is that a human being can alter his life by altering his attitude."

What I have learned is that everything that happens on this planet provides us the opportunity for a deeper understanding of and appreciation for life.

Eckhart Tolle wrote, "Whatever is going on in the moment is okay . . . we really don't have problems, we have situations." thinking?

I can choose to make life okay with my perceptions. Because of the FA and AA programs, I have figured out what matters. A joyful, thankful attitude carries me a long way. A grateful heart does not eat excessively. I can stick with the program long after the desire has left me because I am grateful. There is no room for negativity and gratitude in the same moment.

I used to believe that Alcoholics Anonymous was shortened to AA because what really happened was an Attitude Adjustment. It was really such a simple tweak or reframe for my mind.

I recall my second AA meeting, where I met a woman with four years sobriety. She was very kind to me, but reminded me that I was not to be impressed with her because she was only a drink away from a drunk, just like me.

Wow!!! "Monumental insight" was all I could think. My simple fogged-over, shame-based mind was enlightened forever by that truth. I was told not to whine or complain and to simply do service from day one.

I was put in charge of making coffee for the AA meetings. Imagine that: I had one day sober and my new sponsor told me that I had to take the coffee commitment every day for 90 days. I actually loved it. I had to get there early. People were counting on me and got to know me. I felt like part of the group. After 90 days, I asked for the next assignment and she told me to do it for another 90 days. I happily did it. Such is the lesson of consistency.

If happiness is an inside job, who plans the entertainment?

From my first AA meeting, I was told that happiness is an inside job. What did that mean? I was puzzled. I sort of understood that I was being directed to look at myself for love and joy and not seek it outside from a new boyfriend or clothing item that I had just purchased. But this was rocket science as far as I could tell. How could I become the source of my own happiness?

When I got sober, I had months and months of free-floating anxiety. I did not know what to do with myself. *The Big Book* of AA says that we are so sick that we are like men and women that have lost their legs and we cannot grow new ones. I was pulling myself around by my arms, two stumps at the base of my pelvis, on some sort of skateboard. That is really how lost and overwhelmed I felt at first. I went to my meetings every day because I really was afraid that I had no skills to live without alcohol. I believed that all I had inside was a gaping black hole that only had negative energy in it. I was so full of guilt and shame for so long that I was blind to any manner in which I could cause my own happiness.

I would sit for hours between meetings and wonder when the other shoe was going to drop. I felt like I was waiting to be hit by a car or slapped by an invisible force. I could not relax. I thought the only way I could relax was to drink. Thoughts were spinning uncontrollably in my head like a hamster on a wheel with no particular destiny or value. I frequently felt anxious. I believed the caution that I could be "struck drunk" without any forewarning, so I stayed clear of any place that served alcohol. I let go of all my old

— Can't happen w/o that "Peculiar Mental Twist".

72

friends who drank and caroused. I was out there on a high wire with no net.

Luckily, I hooked up with a sponsor who made me do a pre-fourth step with her immediately. I was only a couple of weeks sober, but she jumped me forward. The fourth step tells us to make a searching and fearless moral inventory of ourselves. My sponsor asked me to tell her anything that might make me drink again.

I told her I was mortified at my behavior when I was drunk. I no longer had complete blackouts; they were more like brownouts. I could recall portions of my behavior and predicaments after I sobered up the next day. All of my memories were steeped in guilt and shame. I felt so damaged and dirty. Towards the end, I did truly "drink over my drinking" as the *Big Book* describes. We addicts get to a certain point and we drink because we are so ashamed of how we acted when we drank and we're attempting to gloss over all the guilt, remorse and fear that are attached to the memories.

In order to live with my disease, I had lowered myself below the level of humiliation. My most painful memory was the day I stopped at a neighbor's yard sale on my way home from work. I was invited for a glass of wine. Of course, I would. I was such a sophisticated person, don't you know? So I started drinking wine with this really creepy neighbor and his wife. He made a pass at me and asked me to have sex with him. I was fortunately very grossed out, even in my drunken haze because he truly was disgusting. So I indignantly left and headed towards home.

It was a bit late, so another disgusting drunk who was with us offered to walk me home. I am pretty sure that this guy lived under a bridge. Seriously, I am not joking. I had seen him hanging around town. How he ended up at this yard sale drinking cheap wine with me and these strange neighbors, I will never know.

Anyway, he walked me home. I was defenseless when I drank. I was such an easy target for predators. Admittedly, I often had my own agenda that always involved getting more liquor once I started. But that night was not one those nights. I tried to say good-bye downstairs at the apartment building door. He begged to walk me up the stairs to my apartment. He begged me to let him go in and stay with me. I let him come upstairs. I lied and told him that there were people in the apartment and that I was not allowed to have guests. Then he would not let me go inside unless I kissed him. OMG!! He was so gross. But, I was scared and drunk. I didn't know if he believed my story about the roommates and I was scared of being raped. He had no teeth and he was dirty and smelly. All I can recall was his toothlessness and I am sure that he lived under a bridge. After the kiss, where he tried to slip his disgusting tongue into my mouth, I went into the apartment and was so embarrassed.

That was my bottom. I am not sure how many days after that that I joined AA, but I know that it was imminent after that episode with the toothless, grubby homeless man. I tried to tell myself that I kind of knew him because I had seen him so often hanging out homeless, but that is only rationalizing. At this point I had absolutely no self-respect.

So, I told my sponsor Gayle about "the kiss." This being the most shameful act of my life (at that moment). I told her this when I met with her at her beautiful apartment on the Potomac. She was gorgeous. She was six feet tall, fit, sober for 10 years and working in a high-powered position within the federal government. She was sparkly and clean. She told me to give it up. What would cause me to drink again if I didn't let it out? So, I told her about it. I felt so ashamed and dirty and whorish. She laughed and seemed to be in disbelief about how bad I felt about the homeless man's kiss. She proceeded to tell me that once she was so drunk that she picked some guy up at a bar and did not realize that he had only one leg until they got into her bed!

It couldn't be, I thought to myself. How could this beautiful, perfect human being ever have had done that? And then I remembered the disease: cunning, baffling and powerful. I saw that one can become shiny and new in sobriety. Gayle was so gentle with me.

She gave me hope that day, hope that I would someday feel whole again.

So back to the concept that happiness is an inside job: I chased everything for a hit, for a buzz, for the thrill. I chased the drink, the job, the man, the car, the yummy stuff, the accolades, the degrees, the house, the furniture, the perfect black coat and the perfect children. I got them all and I got myself right there with no sense of long-term joy. It all left me with my big fat sense of failure and desire for more than my fair share of everything, deserved or undeserved. I did not care. I actually began to understand that after years of chasing "the thing," that the path I needed to take was not a horizontal path. In fact, I needed to be on a vertical path. I needed to be on a path that took me up instead of across.

I finally got it that if I were to ever have an ounce of long-term and sustained happiness, I had to seek something inside that was connected to something much bigger than me and stop the outside quest. Seeking "things" just did not work.

Don't get me wrong, those things worked for a while. They all do, but they do not replace a sense of faith and hope in the things that are unseen and indescribable. For example, learning to sit for long periods of time without eating, drinking, chewing or sucking on something is just one of the simple acts of self-discipline that has changed my life. Planning ahead and serving others became my mantras once I noticed that these two things made me feel secure and happy inside.

As I mentioned a couple of pages back, the *Big Book of Alcoholics Anonymous* says that we are like men and women who have lost their legs. We don't grow new ones. I never grew new legs. I grew new expectations and realities. I changed my old views for new ones that could serve me without a drink or a binge. I learned to sit on my hands and bite my tongue when I wanted what I wanted when I wanted it.

The biggest change for me was with Mike. I thought my husband was the entertainment and that his sole purpose in life was to make me happy! Well, wasn't that what the fairytales say? But, lo and behold, I learned the hard way that Mike is a whole human being, too! He has hopes, dreams and fears. He wants to belong and be loved.

I suffered for years in my marriage without understanding my role and my part. The book called *The 12 Steps and the 12 Traditions of AA* says that we are incapable of entering into a true partnership with anyone. We are too dependent or too demanding. I was periodically dependent and demanding with Mike for the first 10 years of our marriage. I was so unhappy and so was he.

I am happy to report that he did not change a bit. I did. I was given a new pair of glasses in the program to see things through a Creator-shaped lens instead of an Eleanor-shaped lens. That new pair of glasses helped me to see that I am responsible for my own happiness and no one is here to supply the entertainment. What a relief! I cannot change the world, but I can change me.

I now supply myself with endless sources of happiness with my co-creator and Higher Power. Life is so good and so rich and so am I. And Mike is so much happier.

First Things First and then everything else falls into place

There are several slogans on the walls of each of the AA rooms. "First Things First" is one of them. I already described "Easy Does It." There is also "Think, Think, Think;" "But for the Grace of God" and "Live and Let Live." All of these slogans are the foundational principles of Alcoholics Anonymous.

"First Things First" was taken from the concept of "Seek ye first the kingdom of God, and all other things shall be given unto you." This is paraphrased, but essentially the belief is that if I put my Higher Power first, everything else unfolds in due course.

The concept of "First Things First" keeps my life very simple and helps me set my priorities. Since my priority is to stay abstinent and sober, I do keep that priority and I then get to be happy, joyous and free. If I have clear thinking and rational emotions, I have half a chance at being of maximum love and service today. I have half a chance at doing the next right thing and taking that next right action. The self-absorption ratio is low. I am able to access my Higher Self with a clear head and a clear conscience. God's will for me can be described as my higher self or my best self. Living in God's will is doing that which connects me to my fellows versus that which isolates me or makes me afraid of them.

I am profoundly happy when I am acting in love and service. The trick is that when I am helping others, I am not in selfishness, which makes me miserable. So putting the weighing and measuring first, allows me to be in a place to access the power of the Universe, to be a present mother, a productive employee, a good friend, a loving wife and my life is ordered.

Just like the concept of surrender, "First Things First," cannot be said and done. It is a concept that must be practiced over and over again as life unfolds from day to day. I think humans, especially addicts, really like things to be neatly packaged and over and done with.

Unfortunately, that is just not how the world operates. The world throws curve balls and diversions our way nonstop, 24/7. I am very careful to be on guard against falling into the default mode of acting on feelings. With "First Things First," there is no acting on feelings. I act on designated priorities, many of which my sponsor has dictated. Much like the priorities of "program, family, job," I must recall to choose love first in all my relationships. If I have the food in order, the next item falls into place.

I'd like to digress here briefly to discuss the relationship between a sponsor and a sponsee. I am both and most of us who have been in AA and FA for any period of time are also both.

Sponsors have what we want and that is how we choose them. If I am not willing to be accountable to my sponsor and take her suggestions, then I should not be sponsored by that person. If I don't want to take direction, then I go back to taking my own mis-direction and that leaves me fat, dumpy, unhappy, sneaky, scheming and bloated.

Sponsors are considered to be the voice of reason. They are not perfect. We often direct sponsees to others for information.

If I can't help a person, someone else can. We are a network of support.

If someone in FA gets cancer, we tell her to talk with Julie, because she stayed abstinent through cancer treatments. If someone is pregnant, we tell her to speak with Meghan because she stayed abstinent through pregnancy.

We don't re-invent the wheel. We just tell people how to navigate life without alcohol or food, based on our own experiences.

Back to my previous thoughts:

Service is love made visible. Service is a manifestation of the Creator's glory. If I am abstinent, I feel best when I am loving and being and allowing love to enter my life. Connection and love is Spirit. In my disease, I had neither connection nor love. In my disease, there was no God. I worshipped food and drink. I was a lost soul. I cannot thank FA and AA enough for ordering my life. It ordered my life so that I could move forward to a higher level of intimacy with those I love. I could not have done that without the 12 Steps. In fact, I bought the Big Lie for years. The Big Lie was that I was separate, that I did not belong and that I had to go it alone.

I remember the days of self-sufficiency and outsider status. They were lonely and desperate days. If I do "First Things First," I never have to go there again. I never have to be terminally unique or fatally self-sufficient. I do belong and I am like you. I am not different and I am not unique. Today I see that I am golden if I seek the promise of serenity from not taking that first bite or drink.

This has been one of the most useful early tools that was handed to me at my first few meetings. I can only do one thing at a time: This is an idea that I understood in an instant, which happens when the truth is presented. I can only do one thing at a time and I had better pick the top priority and then do the next right action after that!

The first thing that I was instructed to do was not drink, a day at a time. After that, all things were possible. And that is true and it happened to me. I went from a discombobulated, confabulator to an articulate woman in recovery who just did not drink, one day at a time, and her world has changed and keeps changing for the better.

Everything gets better when you are sober. At one of my first meetings, I met a gentleman who was wearing yellow plaid pants, a yellow IZOD V-neck sweater and a beautiful pair of matching shoes. I had never in person seen anyone like this in my life. He had 30 years of sobriety. He shook my hand and welcomed me and then he told me that every day gets better and better, even 30 years later! He had a sparkle in his eye and I had the distinct feeling that he needed nothing and no one. He seemed to be walking on water as far as I was concerned. I wanted what he had. He had confidence and a spark that I could not have fathomed back in January of 1986.

I found that same new information in the rooms of FA. There was great emphasis on program, family and job. "First Things First" meant listen to our sponsors and keep our program commitments, first and foremost. This has truly been a miracle for me. Before FA, everyone else came first, my two children, my husband, my siblings, my parents, my job.

I often skipped meals for myself but made sure someone fed my kids. I had a nanny for eight years because I knew that I could not parent my kids in the way that they need to be parented with consistency and the presence of an adult caretaker. So, I certainly made sure that they were taken care of, but I wasn't doing the caretaking. I had no idea how to care for myself, let alone my kids. FA taught me to take care of myself with "First Things First." I have learned so much by applying this principle.

Since December of 2000, I've weighed 120 pounds give or take a pound or two. I came into FA in September of 2000 and lost all the excess weight within the first 100 days. I have felt beautiful and glorious since the first day that I woke up abstinent from all flour and sugar. Honestly, I can say that the self-loathing that had permeated my life evaporated that very first day. I have felt hope every time I put my food on the scale. Everything has gotten better and better.

Leaving behind alcohol was huge. Contented sobriety from alcohol is a daily struggle. Abstinence from food and alcohol and emotional sobriety is the key. One can be drunk on any substance or person. Emotional sobriety is also called serenity and emotional balance. Leaving behind the drama is very important to emotional sobriety and contented abstinence.

I obviously had to get sober to get to FA. But, leaving behind food did give me that next level of recovery that allowed me to experience true intimacy and joy. I weigh and measure my food, my words and now my life to the best of my ability. Over the last decade, everything else has fallen into place.

This year I turned 48. I got sober when I was 24 years old. I have now officially been in recovery for longer than I had been in my disease. Step by step, I have healed. It all started with "First Things First."

Let Go and Let the Universe Take It

Of course, this is code for "Let Go and Let God." I prefer to use the word "Universe" because it reminds me of how big my Higher Power really is. God feels too small to me. It is the One that has no name that I pray to today and every day. It is the Universal Intelligence and Cosmic Consciousness that I know I can tap into at any second of the day and access millions of data points to create my own type of genius. How great is that?

At Day One, I could never have imagined the who, what or where of it all. In the early years, I had lots of help with this concept of letting go. I experienced many painful lessons of hanging on too long and too tight. Over and over again, I was given the lesson of keeping an open hand and an open heart. The sooner I can remember this truth, the sooner I find relief. Human nature however, is to forget. I forget things right after I hear or read them. Within minutes, I can be back to the same behavior and thoughts. Hence, my constant reminder to myself to "Let Go and Let God."

Life is a series of surrenders; it is also a litany of letting go. Everything I have is on loan from the Universe. It does not belong to me and it never will. Not my husband, my kids, my body. I own nothing. The thoughts in my head are all interchangeable depending on my mood, my physical health and my level of spirit contact. Since I own nothing, I tend to cherish it more. When it is time to let something go, I do.

I am still hanging on to the lime green golf sweater that I wore to my California Bar exam, but I am thinking of letting it go. The Buddhists say to be open to everything and attached to nothing. Open to everything and attached to nothing! I am not sure why I do not get rid of the sweater. I know that because it was my father's, I need to see him in my closet once in awhile. To me, seeing that sweater is like seeing him. I feel like if I ever do get rid of the lime green sweater (which I have never worn since that day) that maybe that would be a breakthrough. Unknown. Maybe it would, maybe not.

Last year when I traveled to Israel, I found some pants that I loved. They were available in many different patterns and types of cloth. I loved them, so I bought a few pairs. When I got home, I realized that I had purchased ELEVEN pairs of these pants! I felt like a bit of a glutton, so I vowed to give them away. I have not done that yet and the trip was almost a year ago now. What makes me do this? I know that it is only "stuff," that it makes me happy for two seconds and then it sits in my closet with my other "stuff."

According to what I have read, Mother Teresa owned a metal plate, one set of clothing and a fork. What drives me to purchase

ELEVEN pairs of the same pants in different colors, patterns and textures? And try as I might to become more like Mother Teresa, I continue to feed the Disease of More. It just changes form. So, I am in a continuous process of letting things go. I have had to let people go, I have had to let thinking patterns go and I have had to let go of my own character defects that I once loved.

Letting go and letting the Universe was my early mantra that has become a part of my everyday life. There is no end to the use of this tool for living. It applies to me and my life as I approach 25 years of sobriety, just as it did from the start. I just have to keep life in perspective and understand that I don't really possess anything anyway, so if something is tugging at me, I can let it go. Nothing will happen to me. I will not disappear into thin air. I will be okay.

CHAPTER 9

The Real Meaning of Recovery and Commitment —Surrender to Life

He who conquers oneself (sic)
is greater than one who conquers a city.
—*TWENTY-FOUR HOURS A DAY, MARCH 27*

The years keep flying by, especially the happy ones. I must say while I was in the disease process, I had years of unhappiness. Since I have been abstinent, I have had no bad years. What I know is that life takes commitment. There has to be a conscious decision to be in my life and to make the best of it.

I was really struggling in my marriage at about year nine, just before I got into FA. I was very unhappy. I wanted to leave my husband and I was convinced that he was the root of all my problems. Luckily for him, I did find FA during the ninth year of our marriage and I had a sponsor who told me to seek outside help for the marriage.

First, I was forbidden to speak ill of my husband at all. So when I was not allowed to run him down, I was stuck with myself and my own mind to address ways to solve the problem of an unhappy marriage.

I remember the exact moment that I decided to be in a happy marriage, when I realized after some therapy, that love is a choice.

It was about my third year into freedom from food when I realized that I had the power to be in a happy marriage or in a desperate and sad marriage. That's when I consciously decided to be in a happy marriage. I was convinced that I had the power to be happy or sad generally and that all I had to do was either *be* happy or *be* sad. I knew that my brain was in charge. I had read stories about great people like Walt Whitman who never said an ill word about anyone or anything. I knew that attitude was everything.

So, one day I applied that same concept to my marriage. In a nutshell, I have been extremely happy and content in my marriage ever since. My husband has not changed. He is still the same man I married: easygoing, a bit "glass is half empty" disposition and does not mind being late. On the other hand, I am fairly rigid, glass is half full and HATE being late to anything. But, rather than dwell on our differences as a negative, on most days, I revel in them as a positive aspect of our long and rich partnership. It is good for our children to see two different people with such diverse personalities be madly in love and form a long-lasting partnership.

The next major epiphany happened when I had been abstinent for about five years and 20 years clean and sober. I was at one of the major international airports, waiting for my flight. I was alone, traveling on business. I recall standing there with all of my luggage when this overwhelming feeling of grace came over me.

Suddenly, I "got it" that *this was my life.* I got it that this was my life and my marriage this time around. That these are my children this time around, my job and my house and my mother and my father—this time around! I got it that it was enough. I got it that I would be in AA and FA for the rest of my life, that I would go to meetings and weigh and measure my food for the rest of my life. I was stunned by the revelation that it was just this time around and that I would have more experiences and more lives in the future. My focus needed to be now and this time around.

I kept thinking that I need to learn what I am here to learn now and that I am here with these other souls for a specific purpose and I no longer feel any urgency or need to be more or achieve more or to get more of anything. It was at this moment that I surrendered to life itself. That was the moment that I felt I could stay in my life until I grow very old and pass over to the next phase of my soul's journey.

This all took place in an airport with people flying in and out to places all over the world. People carrying their stuff and chatting on their phones and reading newspapers. People in the thick of life. I was in the thick of life and I was brought to my emotional knees with an overwhelming feeling of God presence. I got it that day and I have felt that sense of awe ever since. I have felt 100% carried and unafraid and okay that this is my life this time around. I am a servant. I will serve this world to the best of my ability. I will take my life experience and walk one among many until the day I die, my only aim to spread hope and to be a light to my fellows.

Everything looks different to me now. Most of the time, I am in a place of neutrality regarding people, places and things. I can still get riled or feel a little blue, but those feelings are fleeting and they're quickly replaced with thoughts of love, abundance and prosperity.

Since that day, I have not wanted a new husband, a new career, a bigger house or more black skirts. I have been largely content with what I have. I have only really hungered to know Spirit more. I hunger for a closer look at myself and others. I hunger for emotional intimacy, which has always been the elusive goal of my life. I hunger to be of greater service and understanding. Since that day I have been glad.

Since this awakening, my mantra has been:

My soul has no birth and it has no death, my soul is infinite, here for about 100 years, in this perfect healthy form, to love and serve.

CHAPTER 10

• • • • • • • • • • • • • •

How to Be in Sustainable Recovery

Just for today, I will have a program.
I may not follow it exactly, but I will have a plan
that requires self-discipline and accountability.

—*JUST FOR TODAY* PAMPHLET/AA

The 12-Step Program of recovery sets up my day. Working the tools eliminates hurry, worry and indecision around food. This elimination of hurry, worry and indecision about what I'll eat leaks out into other areas of my life so that hurry, worry and indecision are eliminated from virtually every area of my life today. The tools of recovery have ordered my life. They say that order is the first law of heaven.

In order to remain free from obsession and compulsion around food and other self-destructive behaviors, FA tells me what to do from the moment I get up until the moment I go to bed.

Upon rising, I am to get on my knees and say "thank you" to my Higher Power and ask for an abstinent day of love and service. I am then to read the *24 Hours a Day* book, written anonymously and published by Hazeldon. I am to read the meditation and prayer for the day. I am then told that I have to have "quiet time" or meditation for 30 minutes. I am told that I am to be still and show up for my Higher Power before the day takes me and I disappear from the Universal sphere of influence, although today I now know that I am never far from that sphere as long as I remember to listen.

I am then told to call my sponsor and commit my food. I write my food down the night before because I can only have what is already in the house. I cannot wait and go to the store and buy what I feel like eating that day. So the program is about recording, reporting and committing our food each day to the sponsor and then later to my Higher Power.

I am to make three outreach calls per day to other members to see how they are doing and to tell them how I am doing. I am told to eat three committed weighed and measured meals per day. A committed meal is a meal that I wrote down the night before and told my sponsor and my Higher Power I would eat. We do not eat unplanned meals. I cannot change my food plan unless I call my sponsor and get permission. I am to get eight hours of sleep and eat meals four to six hours apart. I am also to eat at a table and not while driving or working or walking around.

I am to attend three committed meetings per week. These are meetings that I say I will attend each week. I cannot change the meeting plan because people get to know me and I am in service. They know they can count on me for help.

I am to read two pages of the *Big Book* before bed, the left side of the page and then the right side and finally I am to get on my knees before bed and thank God for an abstinent day full of love and service.

This formula works. It orders my day, my weeks and my months and not only did I lose weight, but I did so effortlessly, feeling safe and secure the entire time. Eating what I wanted when I wanted made me feel out of control. I did not and could not stop once I started and I never knew how much weight I might gain or lose from day to day. I was never sure if my clothes would fit from day to day or if I would have to buy new clothes because of my fluctuating weight. My day was cleared to be present with the three weighed and measured meals. I found myself with large gaps of time after work and before bed where I once binged throughout the evening and then passed out.

In the evening during the week now, I attend meetings on some nights and on the others when I am home, I help clean up, do homework with kids, prep for the next day, make jewelry (which I never would have had time to do) and I enjoy family time with my husband, children and pets as well. With my food in order, I am destined to be happy, joyous and free. There is no longer any discernable barrier to experiencing joy.

I weigh and measure my food three times a day, so the "drug of choice" is there for me to deal with constantly. I must have this structure or I will soon be rationalizing my first bite, and very convincingly, I might add.

There is no question about weighing and measuring booze. My alcohol addiction had a somewhat different face. After so many years, there is no day-to-day confrontation with alcohol like there is with food, since indeed, we must eat to survive. I have only had alcohol thoughts a couple of times in the last ten years. One of those times was after I had received a death threat in connection with my work. I thought, "Wow! I would really like to have a margarita before I die!" But other than that, thoughts of alcohol rarely surface.

In order to have contented abstinence and recovery, I must endeavor to be agreeable, look my best, be polite and respectful and only speak well of others. I am not to gossip or dwell on the negative. I am not to control or criticize my children or my husband. With these directions, I am called to spread joy and light on the planet. Before FA and AA, I simply would not have made this a daily goal. I would not have been other-focused except to judge others. I had always been so severely self-absorbed that I would have missed the opportunity to give praise and focus on the positive.

Today, I let my children and my husband be themselves. They once felt oppressed by my presence and I began to feel like an oppressor. No one and nothing can grow in an oppressive environment. I am now paying attention to their spirits instead of their report cards and paychecks. My children and husband were always going to be and do exactly what they were going to be and do. I just do not have that much power. But my self-centered attitude made my family miserable, especially Mike.

The *Tao Te Ching* says that if you love it, leave it alone. Anthony de Mello says that if you love someone, detachment is the healthiest way to express that love and the Buddha says to be open to everything and attached to nothing.

That is what this basic lesson tells me: to worry about myself. If I take care of myself and I'm there for others, I do not have to set forth a series of expectations and be so attached to the outcomes that I am miserable and so is everyone around me.

Today I practice paying attention to my family's spirits by loving them and letting them speak to me about whatever they want instead of the old behavior that drove me to only ask my kids about completing their homework and cleaning their bedrooms. The kids once fled when they saw me because they knew the grilling was afoot. No grilling today. Just loving. Soon enough they will leave the nest and I would be very sad if I spent these few precious moments on their case about such meaningless things as clean rooms. I can clean their rooms when they go to college. Dirt and disarray really never hurt anyone.

"Be the change you want to see in the world."
—GANDHI

Because of the 12 Steps I am guided and reminded to be my highest self. I am told to fit myself to the world and not fit the world to myself. Today, my level of suffering is directly calibrated by how attached I am to people, places and things. Attachment results in fear that someone won't do what I want or something will not go my way.

It is said that resentments are expectations under construction. Ninety percent of relationships are in my head. What a concept! Detachment allows me to fit myself to the world as it unfolds around me.

I have learned to be flexible, instead of rigid. Flexible people do not get bent out of shape. If I let go and let Higher Power, I am flowing with the universe instead of fighting an illusory uphill battle.

There is a lot of trust in living like this, far more trust than I would have ever been comfortable with in my fat body. I know that it may be hard to see the connection, but the best I can tell you is that everything is better now that I am in a right-sized body. My ego does not enter the room before I do.

Before FA when I was fat, I could not accept or go with the flow on anything because I was terribly unhappy and in a state of chronic fear, doubt and insecurity. Today I actually have faith that my needs will be met and that no matter what happens around me, that I will be okay. They say that the traumatized child is constantly trying to regain control of her environment so that she will not get hurt again. I totally believe this and see why most addicts are involved in outright control of everything.

Addicts usually do not acknowledge they are out of control. The First Step is a monumental admission. It says we admitted we were powerless over food or alcohol or our drug of choice and our lives had become unmanageable.

Addicts seek to control others and their next hit, so their world becomes very small. If they cannot control others, they get rid of people and then they are left with their drug of choice: how to get it, take it, recover long enough to work, go home and focus on how to get it and take it, in a vicious circle.

The only way that addicts can get relief from this need to control people, places and things is to get out of their own heads, hence they seek an altered state of consciousness.

And then, addicts think if this feels so good to be out of their minds for a bit, more would be better, hence the overdose. "More is better" is the common theme of every addict. If a little bit works, more will work better. The Disease of More is born. Trying to find ease creates a disease of the mind, body and soul that takes heroic efforts to overcome, for the lucky ones that do overcome.

Ultimately, food addicts are totally out of control. They cannot control their food intake, their weight, their loved ones or the world around them. The control they so desperately seek eludes them to the breaking point.

The definition of neurosis is trying to fit the world
to your life, instead of fitting your life to the world.
—WAYNE DYER

Letting the world be and conforming my life to it requires me to live in the present moment. It requires me to be present 100% of the time. If I am living with expectation, then I am not living in the present. I read somewhere that we are to savor the entire catastrophe of life: the good, the bad and the ugly. I know today that in so doing, nothing will hurt me. It is okay to be here now. Not even death can take me out. If this body stops working for me, I know that I will journey on to the next thing that my Higher Power has in store for me. The Infinite is what I am. The infinite belongs to me. Right thought leads to mastery. Calmness is power.

Each day in recovery I try to strengthen my mind in order to stay in contented recovery. I read books and articles that require thought and energy. I commit to challenging my mind, not being a mental loafer. Since beginning the 12 Steps at the age of 24, I have taken this exercise very seriously. I have found that learning and creating are very important to my existence. I crave novelty and if I succumb to what I call my sloth self, I become irritable, restless and discontent. I become a dry drunk and a mad food addict.

My uninhibited soul craves new information, art and excellence in all venues. I read everything and do not believe I have to be in school to develop an expertise in any area. I am also a big fan of audio books so that I can learn as I go to and from work and on long trips in the car and airplanes. I love seeing others display their soulful talents. I do my best to stay away from TV and fantasizing. I believe those to be the indulgences of a lazy and misused imagination. Mental loafing is off limits today. Being present requires me to be sharp and appreciative of the labors of others, whether they are mystical or practical.

In his book *As A Man Thinketh,* James Allen states that our minds are like gardens: If we leave them unattended, they will flourish, but with weeds. If we tend to our minds, we can, like the garden, grow beautiful and abundant gardens of purposeful thought.

So my mind can be full of weeds that can poison and kill all of life, or it can be full of life-giving forces itself, like flowers and fruit trees. It is up to me to fill my own mind. It is irresponsible for me not to fill it with ways to create instead of destroy.

So, the garden grows. It is just a matter of what we want to produce: Both the conscious and the unconscious gardener get results. We have a choice in this matter of what kind of results we want. I choose not to let my mind be overrun with weeds any longer.

If I were overeating or getting drunk, I would have no chance at cultivating my intelligence and connecting to the source of all things. If I am watching TV or reading trashy novels, I have less of a chance of cultivating my intelligence and connecting to the source of all things.

For me, mental discipline starts with my morning quiet time and ends with prayer in the evening. In between is a lifetime of filling my mind with Universal genius and harnessing the solutions to problems for the still suffering.

I have learned to do anonymous deeds and to have a thicker skin in the 12-Step program. It does seem like everything I needed to know I learned by kindergarten. It really does. I remember really early in Brownies (Girl Scouts who are five) that I was told to do something for someone and not get found out. It is no wonder they are called Brownies. Later I learned that a Brownie is a mythical creature that does good things for people without being noticed, like a fairy or a leprechaun. I loved being a Brownie and I loved learning about being helpful. It was in my heart from an early age to be nice and to make the lives of others better.

Remember my childhood dreams of becoming a nun? When I was playing at being a nun, I would wear a long dress and put the towel on my head and walk down the stairs like a powerful agent of God. I am not sure how that got rubbed out of me, but I am certain that this desire to be helpful and saintly never really left me. I just couldn't reconcile it after I became the neighborhood flirt not even a year later and willingly showed you mine if you showed me yours. I was changing rapidly back then due to the family chaos and child abuse.

Anyway, the good deed lesson from Brownies has always stuck with me and it seems like the perfect edict for the alcoholic who is supposed to be anonymous anyway.

I try to do a good turn for someone every day without getting credit. I do the obvious ones like put money in an expired meter for a parked car. I also pray for people and I give things to people I do not know with no expectation of acknowledgment or reward. I do simple things like throw people's newspapers up the driveway and pick up trash when I am out walking the dogs. I really believe that these simple exercises build character and allow me to be a responsible citizen.

I have also learned to stretch myself. Wayne Dyer says that it is lonely at the extra mile because so few people walk it. This means that I go above and beyond to serve my family, my fellows and myself.

Really. I am now clean, sober and abstinent. So if I sign my name to it, it better be a job well done. No more half measures. Living in the world as a mature, pleasant individual is the goal of every person in recovery.

Stepping out of myself makes me feel good and is consistent with the bottom line, which is listed in the AA literature over and over again: My sole (soul) purpose in life is to serve God and others. Stretching myself and going the extra mile, being a creator and not a destroyer give me my daily reprieve.

The other part of this directive is to not show when I am hurt. Addicts suffer from super thin skin. We are so sensitive! Actually, some theorize that we drink and use because we are so sensitive. But, I say bull pucky on that. I just never grew up. I really did stop emotionally maturing when I started using. I was so self-centered and immature that I did not realize that others did not care that much about me so why should I care so much about what others said or did. In a nutshell, I had to get over myself. I was forced to behave like an adult woman and not a big baby.

It took me decades to understand this, but once I finally did, life was much better. The thoughts and words of others cannot hurt me. A whole new level of freedom emerged when I realized that I do not have to care about the opinion of others. I really only need to approve of myself. I know that this is much easier said than done, but practice in this area can bring immeasurable peace and freedom.

Turn out all thoughts of doubt and fear and resentment.
Never tolerate them if you can help it.
Bar the windows and doors of your mind against them,
as you would bar your home against a thief
who would steal in to take your treasures.
—*Twenty-Four Hours a Day, May 12*

....

CHAPTER 11

MYOB
(Mind Your Own Business)

I learned early on to God Bless *Them,* and to Change *Me.* Isabel used to say this all the time at my early FA meetings. She was a kind and gentle woman who reminded me of one of my paternal aunts. She had deep, dark wells for eyes that sparkled and danced when she spoke of her reverence for FA and the fact that she got her life back since walking in the doors.

I did not like this phrase at first. But, later I realized that in my pursuit to mind my own business and keep my eyes on my own plate, that I simply had to stop judging others and save all judgment for myself, if I must judge at all.

This was an eye opener in my early days. I was basically told to mind my own business. I had no idea what my own business actually *was.* Nevertheless I was told to mind my own business. The nice way of saying that was "Live and Let Live," another AA catchphrase. Or another way was to *live simply so that others may simply live.* Nobody cut corners with me. I must not have looked very fragile, although I felt it.

I was told to MYOB (mind your own business, not God's). This was a phrase that I attribute to Marian, an old, old-timer from my hometown. She had lots of famous sayings. This one stuck out foremost for me because I had a lot of work to do around minding my own business.

I had trouble sorting out what was God's job and what was mine. If I was unsure, I would ask my sponsor. The lines got blurry for me in relationships and when I had kids, it was a co-dependent's dream come true. Finally there were little people that I could control! I have learned many hard lessons around the concept of "Live and Let Live," but mostly I am grateful for the edict because I have learned to focus on myself. It was a relief when I was advised that I was powerless over people, places and things and that I had two things in the world that I could control: My actions and my reactions. I thought, "Wow, that's an idea! But what about the rest of the stuff?"

I was so accustomed to living in other people's drama that frankly this concept threw me. I didn't know what to do with my day if I couldn't tell you how to run your life or contemplate the woes of society. I was always focused outward and rarely, if ever, focused inward. Becoming a person who cares about her spirit was completely novel. In fact, when I first got here, I did not believe in any type of Higher Power. I was especially offended by the patriarchal society and literally could not utter the Lord's Prayer. So making this an "inside job" took time and it took pain. The person in the mirror is the only person I could control. I have grown in this area. I now embrace and believe this to be true.

I know that the power is in the present and my happiness is contingent on my right actions. The more I monitor my thoughts, words and actions and not anybody else's, the happier I am. It is so interesting to see that bliss is contained in such a simple truth. When I thought that I was in charge of other people and their lives, it was a huge burden. I was the self-appointed arbiter of the universe with no actual power so I was always miserable and disappointed when everyone else wouldn't act the way I thought they needed to act. When I realized that was not my job, it was a relief. Seeing that I am only in charge of my actions and reactions, which I have the power to change, has been an underpinning of restoration to sanity and wholeness.

Out of survival mode

"Live" is the first part of this phrase "Live and Let Live." "Live" to me has a whole connotation that I simply did not experience before FA. Live means to do more than survive. I was in survival mode before AA and FA. Even in AA for 15 years, I was still in survival mode. Life was hard.

This brings to mind the song *Row, Row, Row Your Boat*. Wayne Dyer mentions it in *There is a Spiritual Solution for Every Problem* and it's the song that I live by today. I am amazed that after eight years of college and graduate school, after studying Sartre, Dickinson and Chomsky and searching for the philosophical answers to life, I found them in this children's song made profound after Mr. Dyer's two-minute analysis.

Row, row, row your boat,
Gently down the stream.
Merrily, merrily, merrily, merrily
Life is but a dream.
—CHILDREN'S NURSERY RHYME AND SONG

So rowing is advised here. I cannot stop midstream and do nothing. In FA, we are often told that we have to do our one percent. Activity is required. The FA preamble tells us that "Action" is the magic word. I must row. I must do my part; I must practice the seventh AA tradition of being self-supporting through my own contributions. I must row. I get that.

But then it goes on to say, "Gently down the stream." How many years did I think that I had to fight for my life like a madwoman to row (or find someone else to row for me) UPSTREAM? Years! I thought I was always fighting an uphill battle and that life was SUPPOSED to be hard.

The first thing I heard when I walked into the AA rooms was "Surrender to Win." I was never supposed to paddle upstream like a Tasmanian Devil. I had it all wrong and here it is in the song. Go gently with the current of life and no longer paddle upstream. That is such a tiring way to live. Just thinking about it makes me so tired. Ahhh . . . what a relief!

Then the song goes on to say, "Merrily, merrily, merrily, merrily." I am supposed to be glad. Just like the Biblical saying, "Rejoice and be glad for this is the day that God has made."

Happily, I must row.

Gladly, I must take action and serve.

With grace and gratitude, I must do the next right thing.

What a phenomenal revelation of epic proportions! There it is in this nursery rhyme.

And the last line, "Life is but a dream." How true! How magnificently true that life is but a dream. And as I learn to quiet my mind and find my way, it becomes more so each day. I am highly overpaid today in every area. I settled for the crumbs of life when I was in my disease. I never thought I would amount to much or that I deserved the love and support of the universe. I felt entitled on my good days and righteously disenfranchised on my worst. Today, I am sometimes guilt-ridden at the gleeful and abundant life that I lead because it feels too good to be true. But, here is the catch: It isn't too good to be true. It is my life.

The FA version of mind your own business is to keep my eyes on my own plate. I love how many ways the 12 Steppers say the same thing in so many different ways, in case I don't get it. It is like one of those psychological tests where the same question is asked in a bunch of different ways in hopes that at some point the person being evaluated will get caught into telling the truth.

In 12 Steps, the same messages are presented in a multitude of ways in hopes that the hardheaded and the degenerated will hear it by accident and the lights will go on. Some of us even pretend that we made up some of this stuff ourselves. I must admit however, that I have no original thoughts. The only thing I have that I can call my own is my own experience, strength and hope. The rest of what I write or say, I heard somewhere or I read somewhere or I saw somewhere. That is the essence of a seeker in recovery. I have filled my life with your stories and understandings because they have given me hope and wisdom beyond my own capacity.

"Live and Let Live" also reminds me of healthy God reliance and detachment from people, places and things. Ralph Waldo Emerson said the following, "Self-reliance, the height and perfection of man is reliance on God."

Abraham Maslow characterized his healthiest subjects as independent, detached and self-governing, with a tendency to look within for their guiding values and rules by which they lived. He also noted their strong preference, even need, for privacy and their detachment from people in general. Maslow called such people "autonomous."

In recovery, I have become centered in that bedrock of wholeness inside of me. How I feel today is not contingent on how you feel. I experience autonomy today. I have worked really hard at detaching from things that limit me and have sought to become one with those things that empower me. Self-reliance for me has come to be a reliance on my Higher or Best Self. I no longer rely on people, places or things to approve of me, save me, support me or make me happy. I feel very alive. I feel whole and on purpose. I am recovered. I have recovered my soul.

Detachment means zero resentment. With a more detached attitude, I can flow through life without judgment about things that are "supposed" to be. I don't sit back and calculate how people, places and things are not how I want them to be. In essence, I surrender my control (which I never had in the first place).

Detachment is not the same as not loving someone or caring about someone or how things are. Detachment is a kind of radical acceptance that allows my love and compassion to have an even greater impact in the present moment.

Detachment releases joy and is the secret to health and peace of mind. It has more to do with what I think and feel and less to do with your actions or my actions. When I become detached from my judgments about you, I am free to align with life on life's terms and how the Universe has presented the situation to me in this moment. This brings to mind the famous Serenity Prayer, "God grant me the serenity to accept the things I cannot change, the courage to change the things that I can and the wisdom to know the difference."

This gives me great relief to accept and move on. It allows me to be light, light on the planet and a "light" to the world.

Choosing to let others live how they want is truly a decision on my part that delivers an automatic dose of serenity. The payoff is almost simultaneous. Several years ago on New Year's Eve, I made a resolution even though I really do not believe in "New Year's Resolutions" because I don't think most people keep them. But, that year I decided I needed some symbolism around my vow.

My vow and my promise was to live the coming year as an experiment, to let my husband be and do whatever he wanted to be and do! I also vowed to be a "doting wife." I made a conscious decision to let God take care of him and to love and adore him.

I had rarely been verbally critical or abusive of him since my sponsor told me I couldn't. But I still harbored an internal monologue of criticism and I still tried to control him.

Since that resolution, I have had a new freedom. I have "let him" make mistakes and help himself with life's lessons in a way that I did not do before. I respect him more and I let him have his own relationship with our children, instead of being the mediator or the intervener. He has grown and we have all blossomed because I left him in the hands of a loving and merciful God. I was so foolish and self-centered to do otherwise and I suffered mightily for that misguided activity. We all did. To "Let Live" required a decision and its reward is peace and serenity.

Mother Teresa said, "People are so preoccupied with the things of the Earth, they have no time for God." Because I have learned to live and let live, I have more time for God. I have stopped dwelling on people, places and things and I have developed a yearning for those things that are not seen. I have developed a yearning for harmony, abundance of spirit, justice and tolerance.

Keeping an open mind is another practice that is essential to the individual in recovery. I've already acknowledged I was Miss Know-It-All when I got to AA. I could not see or hear anything but a series of my own negative and diseased projections. I had to be told to open up my mind. In the rooms of AA, I heard first that a brain is like a parachute: It works best when it is open. I needed that simple image when I first started and I thought letting new ideas in was just too risky for my extraordinarily fragile psyche. Such is the case of the diseased brain.

"There is a principle which is a bar against all information, which is proof against all arguments and which cannot fail to keep a man in everlasting ignorance. That principle is contempt prior to investigation."
—*THE BIG BOOK OF ALCOHOLICS ANONYMOUS*, p. 570

Today these simple principles apply in all domains of my life. I use them in my recovery program, in my family and at work. These principles address tolerance, trust and faith. To have the attribute of honesty means that I do what I say and I say what I do. It means that I lead a transparent life and that I strive for authenticity. To be an open-minded person means to open myself to whatever life gives me on all planes of reality: material, mental and spiritual. It tells me to be teachable, not afraid and detached. Willingness is the key that opens all doors, almost automatically. Willingness is the magic ingredient to all of life's mystery.

In the disease, my default mode was that I was a "know it all." I was suspicious of new ideas or new people. I was not in a place to receive information because I was so closed-minded in spite of an actual belief that I was progressive and liberal. I was rigid and intolerant because I was afraid. If I could control the information coming in, I could be safer, or so I thought.

My disease had convinced me that I was right: I was "better than," while at the same time I was "less than" and I did not belong. My disease convinced me I was different and unique. That is why it was so important for me to accept Step One completely, that I am powerless over alcohol and that my life had become unmanageable. If I do not take Step One completely than I cannot take any direction and I cannot recover. If I have not admitted that "my way" did not work, I cannot take direction.

I had to fold under the weight of my own ignorance, a mighty feat only achievable by the most desperate of humankind. It is a paradox of reality, to be so sure of my position one moment and then, in the next moment, completely sure that I have no idea what I am doing. Only an act of the angels can make this happen. It is truly a miracle that I cracked open that day in Takoma Park, Maryland and then proceeded to do what was necessary to put the pieces back together again.

Once I surrendered and admitted my powerlessness, I was able to take direction. I was on my knees when entering AA and was easily led to the well of knowledge and fellowship.

With the food, it was different. I felt myself balk, argue and want further explanation around the FA rules. But, every time I did that, my sponsor would ask, "Do you want me to sponsor you?" If so, she would go on, "Then you have to follow my directions and you have to be willing to go to any length for your recovery."

Even when I disagreed, I kept an open mind and did what I was told to do. The weight melted off and I gained a little bit of happiness each day.

Since I started in FA, I have not awakened with any self-loathing. Not one day. Since I started being abstinent and following directions, I have felt clean, clear and vital. It took one day of following directions around my food intake. And now it is more than ten years later. I have not had a snack, flour, sugar or unguarded quantities of food since that first day. My armor was cracked. I let the light of FA creep in with Sophie, that gracious lady who showed me that the 12 Steps could apply to food that day at the end of an AA meeting on Waikiki Beach. I have been free of my twisted and deluded thinking about food ever since.

Because I kept an open mind and was willing to follow what I believed at first to be insane directions, I have had the ability to work the 12 Steps and experience a personality change of great magnitude. I am no longer full of fear, doubt and insecurity.

At the age of 38, I learned for the first time do what I was told. That and only that empowered me to conquer my own cravings and desires, placing me squarely in the mainstream of life, love and service. For this I shall always be grateful. Having an open mind saved my life, my marriage, my job, my family and my soul.

Today whenever the trapdoor on my brain wants to slam shut, I have an awareness that I do not know everything and if my reaction is that strong, then perhaps I ought to listen. I do not know what shoes you have walked in. I cannot be hurt by holding my heart open to the Universe. I can only be a better person and a vessel that can be filled with the source of all things and thereby fulfill my purpose in life.

I want to be the Prayer of St. Francis. I live to be the Prayer of St. Francis. For this I shall remain open.

The Prayer of St. Francis

Lord, make me an instrument of your peace,
Where there is hatred, let me sow love;
Where there is injury, pardon;
Where there is doubt, faith;
Where there is despair, hope;
Where there is darkness, light;
Where there is sadness, joy;

O Divine Master, grant that I may not so much
seek to be consoled as to console;

To be understood as to understand;
to be loved as to love.

For it is in giving that we receive;
it is in pardoning that we are pardoned;
and it is in dying that we are born to eternal life.

. . . .

CHAPTER 12

But for the Grace of God, There Go I

I am lucky. I know that there is little difference between myself and the woman in prison for myriad crimes committed to get drugs or to stay high. I am certain of that fact.

I know that I was prayed into AA. I am sure that I came into to AA as an answer to the prayers of those who loved me. In fact, when I told my mother the story of me "getting that moment of clarity" in my apartment in DC that caused me to suddenly phone AA, she kindly informed me that I had called her the night before drunk as a skunk and she told me to call AA the following day.

How is that for direction from the Universe? I actually thought all these years that I thought of it and that it was an inspiration from God. Prayers from my mother and my father no doubt got me to AA. I am not sure that a lost soul can find the way here without someone's love and guidance, be it spiritual or actual. So I know that I was prayed into the 12 Steps.

And I have prayed for others to come to sobriety through AA and FA and they have because prayer works. This slogan causes me to live by two principles: Humility and compassion. I cannot take credit for my recovery. My recovery belongs to my Higher Power and I understand that I own nothing. I am in a state of grace. I am a food addict after more than ten years holding at a 120-pound body, I am a bite away from a binge and I am a drink away from a drunk even after 25 years. I am under God's grace today because I follow the Creator's direction in the form of the 12 Steps.

I learned long ago that I can celebrate my recovery, but that I cannot take credit for it. When I remember to be humble, I have compassion for others instead of judgment and intolerance. I do not wonder anymore why so-and-so doesn't come to FA or do this or that.

I know 100% that each of us is actually doing the best that we can at this moment in time. I really believe that today. Each of us is doing exactly what we are capable of doing at this time. It is true that some of us may be a little further along the path, but it is not true that it is anything but God's grace that allows any of us anything.

> *The attainment of greater humility is the foundation principle of each of AA's Twelve Steps. For without some degree of humility, no alcoholic can stay sober at all. Nearly all AAs have found too, that unless they develop much more of this precious quality than may be required just for sobriety, they still haven't much chance of becoming truly happy. Without it, they cannot live to much useful purpose, or, in adversity, be able to summon the faith that can meet any emergency.*
> —AS BILL SEES IT, PAGE 74

"But for the grace of God, there go I," also puts me in an open-heart position because I am more likely to think, "How can I help?" than to condemn or compare. Above all, staying abstinent is the first thing that I have done to improve the planet. Then with a clear mind and a clear conscience, I can discern how I can help at any time of day or night. I can ask the universe, "How can I help?" instead of "What can I get?" This is a total shift in consciousness.

Mother Teresa said, "It is doesn't matter what you say or what you do, it matters who you are."

That is why her guidance for healing the suffering of others is to be with them, hold the dying, hold the orphaned child, gaze into the eyes of another human being. She called this, "seeing Jesus in all his distressing disguises" in the streets of Calcutta.

Among the Buddhist teachings is the belief that our ultimate purpose in this life is to cultivate compassion. I have found that it is nearly impossible for me to have any true compassion for another human being unless I have compassion for myself and I call upon the Source of All Things to give me the lens of humility. I once mistook pity for compassion. Today I know that pity is arrogant and self-centered. True compassion is kindness and selflessness fueled by a love for humanity that has no bounds.

It is vital that I give the Source of All Things the credit for arresting my disease one day at a time. I have the good sense to know that my daily reprieve from the insanity of my addiction is contingent upon my thanksgiving and gratitude and that I must renew such an attitude every single day. My spiritual fitness is not something that I can take for granted by any means. It is Amazing Grace that saved a wretch like me and for that I will be forever beholden.

• • • • • • • • • • • • • •

CHAPTER 13

Prayer Works

As I pointed out earlier, I was prayed into the 12 Steps. I have also prayed people into the rooms. I prayed in my sister Kay, my friend Pedro, an attorney I see almost every day, who was often "sick" on Mondays and sometimes drunk or recently drunk and at work. I prayed another attorney into FA and a couple of friends and relatives.

When you pray someone into the 12 Steps, that means you don't tell them to go to AA. The exception for me was the case of my sister who wanted to live with me. I told her that she had to go to any 12-Step meeting for 30 days in a row and then she could come and live with me. By the end of the 30 days, she realized she was an alcoholic and wasn't desperate anymore, so she decided to stay and finish college. She is still clean and sober today, almost 25 years later.

Anyway, prayer works. The moment I place my thoughts on a higher plane, everything is okay. I am drawn into the present moment and I can focus on my spirit and things spiritual. The internal noise ends. I am in the presence of the Source of All Things. In an instant, I become God-centered instead of self-centered. What I know today is that every thought is a prayer. I do not believe that the Universe is gauging which of my thoughts is a prayerful thought and which is not. That is why our thoughts are so powerful. They actually say that worrying is praying for what you don't want! Be careful what you think because it just might happen.

I also believe that every action is a prayer. Weighing and measuring my food is a prayer. It is a ritual like the Eucharist. It is my communion. I walk on holy ground. I am in sacred space. I have the power to do great and creative things and I have the power to destroy. Each of my words is powerful and I must be aware to choose them carefully. A strong desire coupled with faith and perseverance can move mountains.

The Big Book of Alcoholics Anonymous is full of instruction on how to pray and when to pray. It tells us to pray for those for whom we have resentments, because suddenly we are transformed by that prayer and no longer resentful. You simply cannot pray for someone and be resentful at the same time. It is not possible. Prayer heals.

My personal favorite proof that prayer works came from my struggle with one of my daughters, who was then 10 and began bedwetting after years of no bedwetting since the age of 2. I was beside myself. What should I do?

I talked to my spiritual advisors and I knew that I could in no way do anything that would make my daughter feel any worse than she already did about the bedwetting. I immediately went through all the negative thoughts about how she must be having emotional problems, or that something really bad happened to her that she was not telling me about. Others pointed out that this happens especially during growth spurts for young children.

At first, I took matters into my own hands. I limited her liquid intake after 6 p.m. I set an alarm at midnight to wake her and take her to the bathroom. I was miserable because I had my first sponsee calls at 5:30 or 6:00 a.m. and disturbing my own sleep was a bad idea. My little one would get up and sit on the pot and dutifully go to the bathroom and I would put her back to bed. I would lie wide awake wondering if she would still wet the bed. Sometimes she did.

I was planning to register her at the Stanford Hospital sleep disorder clinic in order to "get down to the real problem." My head was reeling with how much that might cost and whether my insurance would pay for it and whether I had time to take my daughter to a sleep clinic and have her involved in a study. I was full of fear, doubt and insecurity. It was full-blown self-will run riot. I thought I was just being a good mother.

I would wake up, check the sheets and my whole day would be determined by whether "my way" was working or not. Sound familiar? Needless to say, we were both miserable because of my well-intended control methods.

Finally I got it. I needed to turn the solution and care of my child's "problem" over to God! I needed to surrender the elusive "control" that I thought I had over my daughter's biology and trust that would work it out. I had to have some faith here.

Over the years, I have read Emmit Fox, who is often called the grandfather of Alcoholics Anonymous. He writes beautifully and simply on the connection of the mind, prayer and constructive thinking. He has a whole chapter in one of his books called the "Power of Constructive Thinking" dedicated to realizing a demonstration of God's power through prayer. I needed the recipe. The chapter is short and I read it a couple of times one night before bed.

I was getting ready to give it to God and see if this stuff really worked. God can solve all "problems." The issue is what I believe is a problem that becomes the real point of reality. So, I perceived that my daughter wetting her bed at the age of ten was a serious issue and I could not get the matter out of my mind. I learned in the Emmit Fox book that I had to get rid of all my resentments in order to experience a demonstration of God's healing power.

Only the pure of heart can access the power of the Universe in the manner I needed to access it. Wow!

I had to examine my soul and do whatever it took to rid myself of any ill thought of another human being, institution or organization. So I did that. I identified a couple of people that I was holding grudges against and I let them go in the spirit of 100% forgiveness. I was blown away at the fact that my own house needed to be clean before I could channel my Higher Power's love in my life.

I was then instructed to give the issue of my daughter's bed-wetting to God and to believe 100% that he would create a miracle of healing and that she would stop wetting the bed. I was instructed that I would have doubt at first frequently and then at various intervals. I was to banish all doubt immediately and not to entertain any doubt past the first uninvited thought.

They say in AA that we are not responsible for the first thought, but that we are for the second thought. So I got on my knees that fateful first night and I gave the bedwetting problem to my Higher Power after I was able to come to him with a pure heart. I held my hands open to him and asked him to heal my daughter. I did not set the alarm to wake her. Throughout the night, I woke up and my first thought was doubt and fear that she would wet the bed again. Then I would strike the thought and believe with all my heart that my Higher Power would demonstrate the love and power for my family if I believed in it.

The next morning, she wet the bed. I simply changed her sheets, told her that it would end soon and that I loved her. She was amazed and relieved that this was not a big deal. Then I went back to my blind faith as Emmit Fox had instructed. I did this for the next two nights, always striking any doubts of fear and keeping a pure heart for my love of my Higher Power. The bedwetting stopped on the third morning and has not been an issue since. She is going off to college next year. I avoided scarring my child for life by turning her over to the care and loving grace of the Creator. I cannot tell you that this was anything I would have done if I had not learned the power of surrender and the power of prayer.

When I have a "problem" with any individual at work, I squarely place my thoughts on the Source of All Things and the "problem" or fear completely disappears. Fear and faith simply cannot occupy the same brain frame at once. The Golden Key that Emmit Fox describes is to stop thinking about the difficulty, whatever it is, and to think about your Higher Power instead. It works every time. The difficulty goes away almost immediately.

This is true and available to all of us. Prayer causes me to stop, let go, surrender, trust, think positively and envision the good outcome. My Higher Power knows what is in my heart due to my prayer and placing my thoughts on a higher plane. Prayer changes things because prayer changes thoughts. What we know from so many throughout the ages is that thoughts become things.

Today my life is a prayer. Everything is congruent because I seek to live an authentic and prayerful life. My actions are love and service. My health is excellent due to the disciplines that I have found around my food in FA. My words are loving and compassionate. My words are weighed and measured like my food. My thoughts are kind and tender. I think constantly of abundance, prosperity and compassion. I believe that my purpose in being here is to make the lives of others easier. From the moment I wake up until the moment I go to sleep, I am working on my conscious contact with a Higher Power thereby placing my thoughts, words and actions on higher ground.

The Big Book points out that we are driven by a hundred forms of fear and self-delusion. Ninety percent of life is our perception of life. Life is what our minds make of it. We are conditioned from an early age to cope in this big place called The World. Many of us learned our coping skills before the age of four. Unfortunately, those four-year-old coping skills stop serving us as we age. However, many of us did not have the good fortune of learning more productive skill sets until a situation forced us to do so or we died.

At first I had to depend on the group to help me dispel the bogeyman who lurked everywhere. I also had to live many years in recovery before I got it that the other shoe would never drop. The power behind me is that of the Creator and my fellows and indeed it is a powerful combination that will always keep me safe.

The big lie that we are all separate took some time to be erased, but in those years when I still believed it, it was a real sense of loneliness, isolation and "me against the world." Life situations seemed overwhelming and impossible before FA. I learned by sharing that whatever "problem" I had, someone else had experienced the same problem and did not resort to overeating again to get through it.

I could not escape being one-upped in FA, because I was not the founder and I was not the first member to survive food addiction. People in FA survived cancer, divorce, blindness, death of children, death of spouse, infidelity, failed tests, car accidents, foreclosures, travel, funerals, weddings, road trips, boat trips, earthquakes and job loss. I would not be a first in FA. Thank goodness I would not be the first.

I have always had the experience, strength and hope of my fellows to draw upon in any circumstance. I was told to make an outreach call to this person and that person to get guidance and advice and then I was told to follow it.

When I first got abstinent, I told my sponsor that if I ever got cancer, I would eat. This was on about my third day of abstinence. At that time I was obviously very committed to my disease, to plan ahead this way. I recall her response. She just looked at me and asked, "Really?" No lecture, no attempt to steer me in a different direction. She just had the smile of a Buddha and said "Really?" with a sparkle in her eye.

Then I saw one of my fellows get cancer. She had surgery, chemo and she still stayed abstinent. She is cancer-free still to this day and she is still abstinent. I attended her wedding and she remains happily married to a beautiful man. She is a strong example for me in FA in more ways than she will ever know. Because of her, I know that I would not overeat, even if I got cancer. I believe that she is healthy today because she took care of herself, the way that FA helps us to take care of ourselves.

I realize now, that I do nothing alone, and that I affect everyone around me. Whatever fear, doubt and insecurity lurked for me in the beginning is no longer there. The bogeyman left and was replaced by a Higher Power. Both shoes are glued to my feet today. No shoe dropping will occur. I know this because of a story in *The Big Book* about Dr. Bob.

When a newcomer asked him how he knew he would still be sober tomorrow, Dr. Bob answered that if he did the things that he does today and believes the things that he believes today, then chances are really good that tomorrow he would stay clean and sober.

I say the same.

. . . .

CHAPTER 14

To Thine Own Self Be True

Self examination, prayer and meditations
are the foundations for a successful and happy life.
—BILL W.

To know myself is different than being a know-it-all. To know thyself is an honest decision to live a life of self-examination and a commitment to live from a place of total humility.

As I have said, the 12 Steps and letting go of flour, sugar and quantities brought me back to myself. When I was overeating, I got further and further from myself. I was a stranger in my own body. My body was foreign and I was not even aware of it.

The physical recovery came from weighing and measuring my food and the emotional recovery has come from working the 12 Steps. The emotional recovery has allowed me to grow spiritually. The steps caused me to understand my part in my own life and made me grow up and take responsibility. The steps helped me change so that I could be more useful to my family, community and society.

The Sixth and Seventh Steps direct me to refine my character to be more and more useful and to become serene. These steps are the spiritual instructions for mining the soul. They are life altering when applied. It is very important to understand that one must work the steps in order because they unfold into one another like a treasure map.

Step 6: We were entirely ready to have God remove all these defects of character.

Step 7: We humbly asked Him to remove our shortcomings.

James Allen in his book *As a Man Thinketh,* wrote: "Serenity is the hallmark of a finished character."

Walt Whitman wrote, "I celebrate myself and I love myself." He modeled self-confidence and self-respect, but not in the arrogant way of an addict. Walt Whitman loved everyone and everything. He was other-focused but did nothing less than also revere himself.

We all have three selves. We have the soul, the ego and the body. The addict lives only in the ego, but his actions impact the soul and the body. Ego's desire is for more achievements, awards, recognition, food, drink, lovers, etc. The ego is rarely satisfied.

The soul/spirit yearns for peace long before it even realizes that it does. Spirit is single-minded toward peace of mind and service.

The body is the vehicle for both the soul and the ego. The body is along for the ride. Feeling comfortable in one's body makes a big difference in how one can serve and have a sense of serenity. My body is the sacred temple that houses the Holy Spirit.

The ego gossips, competes, keeps track and schemes. Today I know myself as an addict and I know myself as the spirit from working the 12 Steps. The 12-Step program was a road map back to myself as both spirit and ego. I became very clear on the distinction. I choose to act in spirit as much as possible today and leave the ego behind.

In order for me to be the artist I choose to be today, I must let go of competition and scheming. I must trust the inspiration of the moment and embrace the universal wisdom that pours in when I am clear and present.

When my channel is clear, all things are possible and I know myself. I am one of the lucky ones, to know myself. I count myself blessed to be under no illusions about my weaknesses or my strengths. After I surrendered to win, I embarked upon the journey of a lifetime to seek and know the will of God.

I must say that it has been the greatest journey of my life. I have traveled to at least 16 countries and many of the 50 United States, yet the journey within is the journey where I have discovered the most jewels. This journey has led me to the buried treasures and the secret maps to the everlasting life and even the fountain of youth. I know what I am made of today and I feel like the woman of substance that I had always wanted to be.

Love is the only reality. That's one of the truths I've harvested from this quest to know myself. I have become transformed from the self-centered, know-it-all to a kind, loving and tenderhearted woman. I work on forgiveness every day and long for it to be my default mode, as natural and as automatic as breathing. I imagine that I may be able to say that forgiveness is my default mode when my journey on the planet is almost done. For now to have forgiveness as default is pure aspiration.

I am not a saint. People still irritate me and I have difficulty forgetting about that irritation in the moment. This is especially true for those closest to me. I can still get really annoyed at the loud chewing of my husband or the high whiny voice of my mother when she is depressed.

So there you are: I am human and I have a long way to go. But aspirations are good because they have always transformed me. I know that someday I will not hear the chewing and that I will just love my mother when she is depressed and not care that I might have to take care of her emotionally at times.

Gandhi said that the pure loving kindness of one gentle soul can nullify the hatred of millions. The Course in Miracles teaches us that love is the only reality. Love is what is real. All else is illusion and delusion. Love is what is real. It is what we are, it is where we are from and it is the truth.

Anything other than love is an illusionary view of the world that separates me from you. The Source of All Things and I are one. We are not one and the same, but we are one. We are all connected. We are all the same. Love binds us together and anything else separates us.

I am one with all and anything short of love dissolves this powerful truth and makes me suffer. I suffer because then I feel different, less than, better than or untethered. There is little room for love and ego. Ego's love is possessive and jealous and pushes everyone away and then rationalizes its own actions. Ego blames and takes no responsibility.

Spirit's love is my purest essence and my most authentic self. Ego tells me I will be vulnerable if I forgive, if I love you without conditions and that I will risk something if I am too open. The truth is that the more vulnerable I get, the more I choose forgiveness. The more vulnerable I am, the freer and happier I am, the better my relationships function and I am more effective and productive at work and in the world.

In the state of mind of "nothing to lose" vulnerability, I tap into what is possible instead of limiting myself by what is impossible. I become the co-creator of my life with the Source of All Things. I align my conscience with that of the Universal genius. I align myself with the same genius of Aristotle, Plato, Einstein, Michelangelo and Mother Teresa. It is all out there and it remains even though these geniuses have left this physical world.

Recovery has made me a creator instead of a destroyer. I first acted in self-destruction in my disease and then I went after everybody and everything else.

In recovery, I create. I was born to create and give birth to ideas and to humans themselves. I was created to create, not to destroy.

I am so grateful for the knowledge that love is the only reality. Bill W. calls it a full and thankful heart:

I try hard to hold fast to the truth that a full and thankful heart cannot entertain conceits. When brimming with gratitude, one's heartbeat must surely result in outgoing love, the finest emotion that we can ever know.

—BILL W., *GRAPEVINE* (MARCH 1962)

In the rooms of AA, we hear all the time that a grateful heart does not drink and it does not overeat. A grateful heart is not self-centered. The program helped me to love instead of being suspicious and competitive. I realized that I am here for giving. I must be clean, sober and abstinent in order to realize my mission. My mission is to give.

The Buddha says that an awakened heart is a heart full of love and service. Our *Big Book* says that love and tolerance are our code.

I am loved and I love today. Neither of these realities was possible in my disease. I am awakened. I have been transformed by love for love.

. . . .

CHAPTER 15

The Wild Woman Lives

I n the 12 Steps, I was told that my worst character defects would become my assets. That has been realized for me. As I mentioned earlier, I no longer destroy, I create. That is my truth.

Today I am an artist. I am an artist of people. I have found my voice and the spiritual freedom that I had craved all my life. Because I healed, I see people and I see their potential. I do not let their negative thoughts of themselves impose that same perception upon me.

After many years of working on my own character defects, I have been given great responsibility by society to try to make things right for others, so I take that gift very seriously.

I see possibilities when I meet a person who is broken in spirit because of life's challenges. I see hope everywhere. I make it my business to share hope, shed light and shape society. Like Michelangelo, who took lumps of stone and carved his great visions, I meet the desperate and I see them whole.

I see past the lies, the addict, the sorrow, the child neglect and I go at it with the faith of the Aztec who took his post on the Pyramid of the Sun to drum in the dawn before the sun came up each day. Today I know the sun will rise and spread its sweet light on all of us if we will just look up. Today I know that the human spirit is resilient and given a bit of hope, souls come back from the dead.

After a time of perseverance, these broken folks do emerge whole, they emerge responsible citizens and they emerge knowing themselves, just like I did. They emerge forever changed by the encounter. Picked off the heap of tragedy, they become newly born humans. Every day, I am passing it on. I have gone from a self-seeking wretch to a recovered woman spreading hope and doing service.

There are so many lessons. Every day that I stay present, which means clean, sober and abstinent, is a day longer and more wonderful than I could have ever imagined. I learned so much from my father and his journey out of alcoholism with the 12 Steps. There are no accidents. The universe is perfectly orchestrated and I was meant to be exactly where I am.

I spent years before claiming recovery for myself, living with the person that I have come to consider one of my greatest teachers, my dad. I will be forever grateful for all that he taught me. I learned from his addiction, his relapses and his recovery. I had a front row seat to the human condition that my father so well embodied in all its imperfection. My dad schooled me in failure and redemption.

Throughout my life, the Creator has called me to be in a complexity of situations. These are not just situations that I envisioned or imagined for myself, but the entire scope of life and all its glory. Along the way I have struggled mightily with career, parenting, marriage and other relationships. I have been forced to grow in many ways that I would rather have not. But, in the end, what is the saving grace is the absolute knowledge that I am more than the material. I have had to actually learn to watch what I pray for because I really will get it.

I am forever grateful and indebted to the 12-Step program for taking me in, even though I was kicking and screaming. Recovery asked nothing in return and has now given me a new life. Due to the radical surrender of people, places and things that made me sick, today I have a connection to the Infinite and a fellowship of sunlight. I seek each new day as if it were my last and I constantly prepare to do the work of love one day at a time.

I have truly surrendered in order to be saved. The wild woman lives and she dances and she drums and she prays and she changes everything she touches and everything she touches changes. I am out of the box.

About the Author

Eleanor R. lives in California with her husband of 19 years and two teenage daughters. She is a faithful member of Food Addicts in Recovery Anonymous and Alcoholics Anonymous. She works each day helping families heal from the devastation of drug and alcohol abuse, trauma and mental health disorders. She has a dog, a cat, two birds and one fish.

Visit her website at www.diseaseofmore.com.

COMING IN 2012...

The story of Eleanor R.'s recovery continues:

Burning Bushes
by Eleanor R.

STEP TWO: We came to believe in a power greater than ourselves and that we could be restored to sanity.

"For some of us, as we enter recovery, it is really difficult to believe in a Higher Power. Admission of our addiction and our inability to conquer it alone is the principle of Step 1 of Alcoholics Anonymous. Hope is the principle behind Step Two. Mustering up hope is a tall order for those of us who feel degraded and unworthy. In fact, it was easier to don the armor of ego each day to protect myself from the pain of believing and then being disappointed than it was to allow myself a glimpse of salvation. I was not sure that hope applied to me.

I needed a God of evidence, a burning bush or a guarantee. I couldn't go on faith. I was too broken. It hurt too much to act on faith. So when I walked into the rooms of AA, I was told that I did not have to believe in God, I just had to believe in a *power greater than myself.* I was offered <u>G</u>roup <u>o</u>f <u>D</u>runks and <u>G</u>ood <u>O</u>rderly <u>D</u>irection. I was told to use the group's belief if I didn't have any. I was told to let them love me until I could love myself. These were watershed moments for me that changed the course of my life. I had neither belief nor love for myself when I walked into my first meeting. I did know one thing: I was home and I wanted to believe in *something.*"

Eleanor R.'s story of addiction and recovery continues in ***Burning Bushes*** as she finds faith and hope while making her way through the second step of AA.

9495582R0008

Made in the USA
Charleston, SC
17 September 2011